MEMOIRS OF A BARBED WIRE SURGEON

Caricature of the author in 1945

Memoirs of a Barbed Wire Surgeon

by Elmer Shabart M.D., F.A.C.S.

REGENT PRESS
1997

Book design, cover design and cover illustrations
by Joseph Stubbs

Edited by Claire Burch

Library of Congress Cataloging–in–Publication Data

Shabart, Elmer, 1909-
   Memoirs of a barbed wire surgeon / by Elmer Shabart.
     p. cm.
   ISBN 1–889059-02-1 (paper)
   1. Prisoners of war--Philippines--Biography. 2. World War,
1939-1945--Prisoners and prisons, Japanese. 3. Prisoners of war-
-United States--Biography. 4. World War, 1939-1945--Personal
narratives, American. 5. World War, 1939-1945--Medical care-
-Philippines. 6. Surgeons--United States--Biography. I. Title.
   [DNLM: 1. Shabart, Elmer, 1909- . WZ 100 S515 1996]
D805.P7S44 1996
940.54'75599'092--dc20
DNLM/DLC
for Library of Congress   96-31856
                                         CIP

Manufactured in the United States of America
Regent Press
6020A Adeline
Oakland, CA 94608

Dedicated to my wife Louise

CONTENTS

A PURPOSE

Not for the sake of the gold,
Not for the sake of the fame,
Not for the prize would I hold
any ambition or aim.
I would be brave and be true,
Just for the good I could do.
I hoped I would be useful on earth,
serving some purpose or cause,
Doing some labor of worth,
giving no thought to applause,
Thinking less of the gold or the fame
than the joy and thrill of the game.
Medals their brightness may lose,
Fame be forgotten or fade,
Any reward I may choose
leaves the account still unpaid,
But little happiness lies
in fighting alone for a prize.
I had the thrill of the task,
The joy of the battle and strife
of being of use, and I ask
no greater reward from this life,
Better than fame or applause
is striving to further such a cause.

Anonymous

ACKNOWLEDGEMENTS

Special recognition is given to

The unknown artist who drew the caricature of me in POW camp in 1945

The unknown author of the poem "A Purpose"

The statements by Gregory Rodriguez in the Journal of Ex POWs

The typing by Marcy McGaugh of Writer's Rescue

"American Defenders of Bataan" and "Secrets of Japanese Tests" by Thomas Easton, repeated by Rodriguez, from The July 1995 issue of *The Quan*

Colonel Eugene Jacobs for permission to copy photos from the Time Life Book Prisoners of War, 1981

Claire Burch for her untiring work in the editing of the manuscript and without whose expert help this book would not have been written

Photo Copy for its skilled help in preparation of the pictures

Regent Press for its excellent preparation of the book

INTRODUCTION

his is a book by a survivor of the Bataan Death March in World War II who managed to continue practicing his profession all through their long ordeal, without instruments, anesthetics, antibiotics, medicines or even simple supplies like bandages and antiseptics.

Dr. Shabart, first as a young man who takes his Hippocratic oath seriously, later as a surgeon reflecting on how they somehow managed to stay alive, takes us on a frightening and revealing journey that begins before the fall of Bataan and actually carries us through to the present.

A fellow prisoner with a gangrenous appendix about to burst, is operated on by Dr. Shabart who knows there is no alternative—without surgical intervention he will surely die of peritonitis. The operation proceeds as many he must do during these years of captivity when civilized medical equipment is not available to him. First he finds a piece of glass sharp enough to use to make an incision. Someone has a spool of thread and a needle. He boils it all and several men hold down the patient who is requesting surgery, knowing it is his only chance. The man lives, recovers, along with many others treated by a doctor who proves as ingenious as Robinson Crusoe on his desert island.

A series of hair raising adventures, none of them for fun, add up to a saga of war-is-hell courage and endurance. One of the lucky ones who gets home after the surrender, this compassionate ex POW has woven a tale of bombings, hurricanes and jungle problems with a passionately ironic almost end—when the war is over he is made a present of two huge cases of finely crafted surgical instruments which had been in the possession of their captors all along. Eventually he donates them to the Army Medical Museum.

Mysteries lurk in this book, questions of Army Intelligence investigations into a possible deal struck in connection with war crimes such as the rumored injections of plague given to POWs at the infamous Unit 731, other atrocities, and little known facts about the American military urge to be one up on all enemies in possible chemical warfare.

The author comes home to a loving wife and excellent offers at further training, eventually becoming the first person to do research and publish a paper on the possible connection between cigarette smoking and lung cancer.

His brushes with death and encounters with deprivation have served to motivate him to continue working and studying towards his goal, improving thoracic surgery. Historic events and tales of quiet heroism are included in this modest story of a life well spent.

C.B.

Before the War

When I was about to begin private practice in 1934, Dr. Karl Schlaepfer, one of the leading surgeons in Milwaukee, Wisconsin, approached me to see if I would join him as his assistant and associate. Karl was a master surgeon, an excellent teacher and a real catalyst, encouraging me to achieve. As a result of this wonderful turn of events, I declined a fellowship in surgery at the Mayo Clinics.

Much later, after the events of this book, in fact after I returned to the United States, he wrote a letter of recommendation for me. I was seeking an appointment in surgery at the Hines Veterans Hospital in Chicago. It was an appointment that could make me eligible to take the examinations to become a certified specialist in my chosen field.

In 1940, I was receiving constant letters from the military to serve one year. It was a time when doctors were badly needed to take care of the increasing new recruits.

I talked it over with Karl and we decided it might be just as well to take one year to help out and get them off my back. I could then return to our practice. In December, 1940 I took the step. Only after I was in the military, I found out that it was not going to be just one year. While in Georgia, eight of us were selected to take our pick serving either in the Philippine Islands or Iceland. We raised a ruckus. One of the eight doctors found that the Articles of War state, "No reserve can be sent outside the continental United States if we are not in a state of war." We confronted several officials with this information, including the Adjutant General in Washington. The answer was, "You're in the army now. Take your pick or you will

receive direct orders." Seven of us decided on the Philippines,
because we felt we would be on the other side of the world
from where the war with Germany was taking place.

The Philippines - Before Hostilities

I arrived in the Islands in August of 1941 aboard the
President Cleveland and was assigned to Fort McKinley,
12th Medical Regiment, Company A, Philippine Scouts.
Many years before, General MacArthur had established
these Scout Units. The Scouts were very proud of their
heritage and were well respected by their fellow citizens.
They were proud and showed their dedication during
battle and later.

I had a very close association with the men of this
company. As time passed, our 1st Sergeant, Sgt. Calm,
became a buddy. He was very dedicated to all his officers
as well as the enlisted men.

Chapter 1
December 7, 1941 War Begins

"At any given moment, life is completely senseless, but viewed over a period, it seems to reveal itself as an organism existing in time, having a purpose, tending in a certain direction.

Aldous Huxley

With the outbreak of war, we were ordered to dismantle all metal in the barracks and discard it in the Pasig River. This river flowed through the very heart of Manila. We were then ordered out of Ft. McKinley which was located about 30 kilometers from Manila.

The defense of the Philippines had been well planned many years before. There was to be a Southern and a Northern Force. After delaying tactics, the plan was to retreat into Bataan and further cause a delaying action until reinforcements would arrive. I guess on paper these tactics appeared very sound and practical. Living it was something else! Those troop movements remain a picture in my brain even today.

We were ordered to give necessary care to the troops who were to defend Subic Bay, one of our largest Navy installations. Unfortunately, when we were trying to move north towards our destination, many other units were also trying to move northward. This caused crisis, confusion and delays. The road was only two lanes and a good portion of it was so dusty you couldn't see one block ahead. It took hours to cover ground that should have taken about thirty to forty-five minutes. Yes, there we sat in our command car at the head of our company, inhaling dust, coughing, eyes watering. As we tried to move along, slow as it was, we wondered why the Japanese didn't strafe that road—they could have knocked out a good portion of our troops. As dusty as it was, we were watching for them. Fortunately, they never came.

Road Military Police were not very helpful either in trying to give directions. We finally stopped on the road to Subic Bay and set up a temporary aid station, finding out that we were about 3 kilometers from Subic Bay.

After spending the night there, we were told to proceed north to Bataan. Getting there we saw the same traffic mess. After hours on the road, again, sunk in chaos and confusion, we finally got there.

We'd been told to set up to the south of the Calumpit bridge. That spot was to be held at all costs so the Northern forces could cross it and join the southern forces. To our surprise, we had no casualties. Not one unit was lost in this delaying action at Calumpit. We did have some stragglers—Filipino soldiers who came into camp while looking for their units. We couldn't help—we ourselves didn't know what was ahead. In this maneuvering, the Northern Forces lost about 10,000 Filipino soldiers due to desertion.

As result of all this turmoil, a word was invented, "SNAFU." Translated, it meant "Situation normal all fucked up."

Eventually, we were ordered again to proceed to Corps One and set up somewhere midway between Bagac and

Mariveles along the Bagac road leading to Mariveles. We again found a suitable area and set up for action. Finally, here we started to get wounded and sick men. Most were malnourished, and ill with either dysentery or malaria or both.

It is a little known fact, but Bataan is considered one of the worst malaria infested areas in the world. At the start of hostilities, all forces were given one five grain tablet of quinine a day—sort of a prophylactic dose, if you can call it that. However, this procedure was discontinued after about a month since the supplies were nearly exhausted. At the start we received wounded who mainly suffered from small arms fire. There were very few with shrapnel injury.

The Bataan area was divided into two Corps. The first encompassed one half of Bataan on the China Sea side. The other half was covered by Corps 2 and bordered on the Manila Bay side. Each Corps had a collecting station to back up and receive the sick and wounded from the Battalion Aid Stations at the front line. The collecting station would offer what medical help it could. If more intensive care was necessary, we would transfer the patient to the Base Hospital in the vicinity of Mariveles. The road was tortuous, and again very dusty.

The Philippines Scouts in my unit numbered between 40 and 50. These men were all trained Corpsmen except for the cooks. They took real pride in what they did. On a busy day we'd get from twenty to thirty wounded or very sick men. Supplies and food were short, for patients, for the company, for all of us. We were finally cut to one-half ration twice a day, with a rare ration of horsemeat. The daily rations probably ran between 1000-1500 calories per day, hardly enough to sustain energy to do the—

work—everyone was malnourished even before being captured.

One day it became necessary for us to visit Corps 2 about supplies. Dr. Arnold Warshell and I did so with the command car. Getting back we came under artillery fire. In passing a church we noticed some Filipino soldiers outside the church, motioning us to come to them. It looked like some were wounded. We took care of them and told them we'd get help. As Dr. Warshell was bending over to take care of a wounded man lying outside the church door, a shell landed nearby and a fragment hit him in the buttocks. He yelled, and I removed the fragment, which fortunately had not gone too deep. On the rest of the trip back, Arnold had a very uncomfortable time sitting, as you might imagine, but, in a matter of about five to seven days, he had no more irritating problem.

One day we had a meeting with our Non-Commissioned men to see if we could somehow better our rations and our patients. The first idea brought up was to get fish. How? The men assured me a small detail of five would go with me to the China Sea shore. Here the men jumped into the water and swam into cave-like structures, which over many years were created by the ebb and flow of the waves. Every once in a while, a Scout would surface and throw a beautiful tropical fish on shore, a fish he'd cornered in the cave and caught with his bare hands. If I hadn't seen this with my own eyes, I would never have believed it possible. When we returned to the Unit, our cooks prepared the fish, and we, as well as our patients, had a delightful meal. They couldn't believe that they were really eating fish. An interesting feature of these fish was that they had no scales. I had never in my life seen a fish without scales. These fish with their dazzling bright colors were really beautiful. I might add that they were also good eating.

One day my Corporal came to camp all excited. He was able to kill an iguana lizard while returning from an Aid Station. All the Scouts were excited and assured us that the meat tasted exactly like chicken meat. We anticipated another worthwhile meal, only sorry to say, the American Officers didn't agree. To us it was in no way near the taste of chicken, but protein is protein, no matter how you get it.

At times we would go out to try and shoot monkeys in the trees. This was difficult because these monkey families seem to have sentries who would alert others to approaching people. However, we did manage to get a couple or so at times. Their meat was not too bad to eat—or maybe we were just hungry!

The other American officers in Company A were Dr. Waters, Dr. Pizer and Dr. Warshell. The four of us grew together with time as though we were brothers.

How did we keep clean? Midway between our Company and Bagac a beautiful mountain stream crossed the road. Although it appeared crystal clear, we knew higher up on the slopes of the mountains it was under contamination from the natives who lived on the slopes. We used it anyhow, being very careful not to get water into our mouths. It was a refreshing delight.

Chapter 2

Problems at the Front Line

"Without a measureless and perpetual uncertainty,
the drama in human life would be destroyed."
Winston Churchill

At one point in time, we suddenly were not receiving any patients from the First Battalion Aid Station. We thought maybe they had been overrun in battle. Sgt. Calm and I took off through the jungle, following a trail to the Aid Station. While on the trail we suddenly were fired upon by a sniper. He missed, as we ducked behind a huge banyan tree. We drew our .45's, and by a decoy maneuver of Sgt. Calm we were able to locate him in a tree. We both fired and he fell. We were lucky, but quite nervous. Could there be more? When we arrived at the Aid Station without further incident, we found out the reason for a lull in their work. The entire unit had been under a heavy artillery barrage that stopped shortly before our arrival. Satisfied, we returned to our camp with no further trouble.

Around the first week of April, I was called to Corps Headquarters. I was told to move my Unit to Corps 2 in the dead of night over a trail that our engineers had previously cut on the North side of Mt. Mariveles. The trail was barely wide enough for a vehicle. I was told it was very dangerous, with steep, high slopes on one side and deep, sharp cuts on the other. The reason this had been cut, so I was told, was to give a communication way to each Corps if other roads were blocked.

I was also told that in the front line of that corps, a heavy barrage had been sent in to try and break the line. It was tremendous, and many casualties were expected to arrive to the rear. Artillery fire was so heavy that a soldier did not dare raise his head out of a foxhole for fear of having it blown off. We knew our help was necessary. The line did indeed give way, and the Japanese began to infiltrate behind our lines.

We broke camp and in the dead of night (no moon either), we set out to find the trail and begin our crossing. The trail was as bad as had been described to me—maybe even worse. We couldn't use our headlights, but just the blue lights, which hardly showed the trail.

As we were slowly proceeding, we rounded a curve. Something was ahead of us. At first we couldn't make it out because of jungle darkness. It stood motionless. Suddenly we realized it was a Japanese tank blocking the trail. We stopped instantly but almost at the same time small arms fire started up from the slope above us. We hollered to hit the downward slope and take cover. Then I crawled along the slope to the last vehicle and started to back it up. The other officers and Scouts did the same with the other vehicles. The command car in front was completely shot up, and we had to leave it. Incredibly, we were able to back up to a safe area where we could turn around and head back to our previous site. Talk about surprises, the only loss was the command car. These days I still think of it as a miracle.

When I returned to Corps Headquarters and reported

the incident, they were amazed—no one had been aware that the enemy had infiltrated so far into our rear, including a tank. They told me to return to the Unit and await further orders.

Chapter 3

The Surrender of Bataan Announced

"Life can only be understood backwards, but must be lived forwards."

Kierkegaard

Though *it was becoming* more and more obvious that the expected help was never going to come, we had no idea why. During the war we were constantly told over the air that reinforcements were on the way—that the sky would be filled with our planes. This was our hope. While we were cut off in Bataan, the Japanese had free flying over our areas. We had nothing to put into the air to challenge them. It was desperate and getting more so.

One day a messenger came to our Unit and asked me to report to Corps Headquarters. I jumped into an ambulance and took off. When I arrived, I was told that General King had surrendered our forces to the Japanese. I was to take the Unit down to Mariveles and surrender them intact. What bad news! Of course, it shouldn't have been a surprise, especially the way events were taking place. Still we'd hoped it would never happen.

I was told by the adjutant that I'd been given a Silver Star medal. At the same time I was handed some papers and told to write myself up. I replied that I wouldn't write myself up—if they thought me worthy of the decoration, they should write me up. The adjutant then told me that the Unit was granted one silver star and if I wouldn't write myself up, I should give it to someone else in the company. I proceeded to write Sgt. Calm up for the medal, finding out much later that Mariveles, Kilometer Post #1, turned out to be the starting point for the infamous Bataan Death March.

Driving back, I was heartbroken. It felt like the end had come! I was also scared. We all were. What to do now—turn in those loyal Scouts to face uncertainties— and what about us four officers? I got an idea about these wonderful Scouts. I knew I was disobeying an order, but it couldn't be helped. I had all the men called together and said to them, "I can only give you fifteen minutes to think this over. Do you want us to surrender you to the enemy, or would each of you want to hit out on your own? There are plenty of Philippine civilians who followed us into Bataan. You could ditch your uniform, borrow some civilian clothes and march out of Bataan with the rest of the civilian families. "I leave this decision to them," thinking I'd probably never see them again.

When I got back in fifteen minutes, Sgt. Calm told me they'd taken a vote, and every man wanted to take a chance going out as a civilian. To satisfy myself, I asked for a show of hands for all those who wanted to go it alone. They all raised their hands. I then told Sgt. Calm to take what rations we had left, divide them equally and set the men free with our very best hope for good luck for all.

Returning I had a sad meeting with Drs. Waters, Pizer and Warshell. A few weeks before, when Sgt. Calm,

Dr. Waters and I were free, we went down to a China Sea beach, and (with Sgt. Calm's know how) built a bamboo raft. The idea was that if we ever needed it, we would sail across Manila Bay at night to a small inlet on the island of Mindoro. The Sergeant knew a civilian fisherman there who had an old motor launch and would gladly give it to us if and when we needed it.

We didn't stop to think of the odds against our ever reaching the place. The enemy at sea—patrolling—the uncertainty of the sea itself, the probable weakness of this raft that we'd only tried out in the calm waters of the bay, and finally, sailing blindly in the darkness of night to a new destination without even a compass. All those problems were things we never talked about.

Chapter 4

An Attempted Getaway

"The truth that many people never understand,
until it is too late, is that the more you try to
avoid suffering, the more you suffer, because
smaller and more insignificant things begin to
torture you in proportion to your fear of being
hurt."

Thomas Merton

During the meeting with Drs. Pizer and Warshell,
no one had other ideas, but finally both doctors
thought they had a better chance by turning
themselves in at Mariveles. It was really hard for all of us
to say goodbye—we hugged in tears.

They finally got into an ambulance and took off. I can
still see them waving back. One moment we felt close
enough to be brothers, the next we were saying goodbye,
maybe never to see each other again, no one knowing
what lay ahead.

Sgt. Calm picked up a 50 mm Browning automatic
(we had them too), and the three of us strapped on our
.45's and ammunition, packed the little rice that was left,
and took off. In our fright and hurry we completely for-
got to take any of the medicine we had in camp, specially
for dysentery and malaria.

When we got to the raft, we put up the sail, and
pushed it into the water. Once into the bay, we were

satisfied it was going to do its job. We then went back to the shore, loaded the little food and water we had, and settled down on the beach until it got dark.

As we sat talking over the trip we were about to start, Sgt. Calm suddenly shouted, "Sirs, look out to sea." There was a cruiser that appeared to be unloading many marines. At the very moment, a Japanese reconnaissance plane came over us, tipping its wings obviously to the cruiser. We thought we might get strafed, but the plane went on and made a turn. We jumped up and headed for the tall beach grass where we could hide. When I threw myself down, I didn't know I was going to land right next to a sleeping iguana. He got as startled as me and took off like he had been shot out of a cannon. As I lay there I thought, if I'd landed just one to two feet to my left, I would have landed square on his back and could have gotten a hell of a ride for a bit. This iguana was taller, or I should say longer, than my height—I would guess he was seven feet long.

When the plane disappeared, we looked out to sea and, sure enough, small boats were just starting to turn into the bay in our direction. We immediately headed for the jungle and the mountain slopes. After running at top speed through rough terrain, we finally sat down to rest, figuring they wouldn't be able to trace us where we were. Finally, we moved a little further into the jungle and took another break to talk over what might come next.

Sergeant Calm suggested that we head north through the steep ravines of the mountain and the dense jungle. He said he knew the head hunters and their dialect. He also knew where they were in the Zambali Mountains, estimating that it would take approximately ten days of tough going to get there. We couldn't follow any trails in case the Japanese would be patrolling them. We spent some time talking about it, and finally Bill (Dr. Waters) and myself agreed. What other choice was there but to surrender? This was the last thing we wanted to do. And Sergeant Calm told us he was sure we'd be able to get medicines with contacts in the valley below.

We took off and finally made it to the top of one ridge. The going was tough because of the steep ravine and the thick jungle with its vines, snakes and animals. Sgt. Calm said, "We have to make two ridges each day—not counting the one we're standing on."

It was late in the day, so we decided to sit tight until daybreak. It wasn't a good night. All those strange noises, eerie darkness—we couldn't even start a fire for fear we'd be detected. I don't think Bill or I slept more than one hour all night long. It was terrifying, and I must say that sunrise never looked so good as it did the next morning. Besides all the animals and snakes, there must have been hordes of mosquitoes who found us. They fed off us all night.

We weren't ready to give up yet so that morning we headed out again. We first tried to let ourselves down a slope, crossed a small creek that was running in the ravine, and started climbing up the slope to the next ridge. The vines were thick, but they did some good—at least we could hang onto them to pull ourselves up or keep from falling backward. Of course, it was hot and humid—this added to our discomfort. The stream at the bottom of the ravine was a savior in that we could cool off somewhat with the water. Since we couldn't drink it knowing it was contaminated by tribes up in the mountains, we filled our canteens but used water tablets for disinfecting it. These were the only pills we'd taken with us.

The object was to make two ridges before nightfall, but on our first day we managed to make only one. We were exhausted and disappointed that we hadn't made the second ridge. This struggle continued for seven or eight days. Unfortunately, each day, no matter how hard we tried, we made only one ridge. Through all this climbing Sgt. Calm managed to still hang onto his heavy Browning automatic.

Finally, one night, as we were trying to relax our sore muscles and bones, Bill and I talked it over and felt we had enough. We could never make it at the pace we were going and chances of us contracting malaria or dysentery were too great. It had been a tragic mistake leaving the medicine back at camp.

We decided to turn ourselves in the next morning, but when morning came, it was hard to break the news to Sgt Calm. Tears welled up in his eyes. He begged us to carry on with him, again assuring us that he'd get us to the hunters, and if we needed medicine, he'd somehow get it.

When we finally told him we just couldn't go on, he discarded the Browning and ammunition, asked us for our .45 revolvers.

Chapter 5

The Japanese Preparation for Bataan

"And how am I to face the odds of man's bedevilment and God's? I, a stranger and afraid In a world I never made."

A. E. Houseman

After we said goodbye, I remembered something my Scouts and I had seen at the time we went down to get fish for our unit. I could almost see those amazing caves created by the waves. Some of the caves had ledges deep inside them. Before the outbreak of war, the Japanese had somehow managed to store artillery pieces in these vast caves. They were well covered with cosmoline to protect them from the salt water. This must have been done in the dead of night under complete darkness, probably even sneaking them into the areas with submarines.

Before the surrender, when I had mentioned this at headquarters, they acted as if they knew and if action was to be taken, it would be too late. We had no way to get to them by sea. Some of the points had coast artillery pieces, but I didn't know where or how many.

Before the outbreak of war, while having dinner one night at the Army-Navy Club in Manila, an officer who had been in the Philippines for several years had casually mentioned to me that, in the event of war, a plan had been made called "WPO-3." As I was told, this seemed to be a delaying action until all forces were in Bataan and awaiting reinforcements. I also was told that he'd heard that it may have been called the Orange Plan. He said a Filipino who knew of the plan had sold it to the Japanese some time before the war. He wasn't sure whether WPO-3 was set up after the Orange Plan had been dropped or whether WPO-3 was the very same as the Orange Plan. Sadly, I never did find out. We just carried on with numerous maneuvers as though nothing would ever happen.

Chapter 6

Dr. Waters and I Surrender

"Those who expect to reap the blessings of freedom must, like men, undergo the fatigue of supporting it."

Thomas Paine

Bill and I knew the general direction of the road which led to Mariveles. As we made our way to it, we carried a white cloth on a small branch. I don't remember how we got it. One time we came upon a twenty foot long python hanging from a branch of a banyan tree. We sure didn't hesitate detouring around it.

When we finally got to the road, we were greeted by a lone Japanese sentry. He searched us, taking all our jewelry, wedding rings, wallets and anything that suited his fancy. He even seemed to enjoy the pictures we carried in our wallets. When he told us to sit down and take our shoes off we wondered, now what? He then took American dollars, gave each of us two, and motioned for us to stick them in the toe of our shoes. Then he motioned us to go towards Mariveles.

After walking about three kilometers, we came upon a squad of Japanese who appeared to have trouble figuring out how to start a huge army eight-wheeler truck. The squad was led by a lieutenant, who immediately flagged us over and made it clear that he wanted us to start the big rig. We figured out they were a salvage crew. He made no bones ordering us to start the truck and drive it for them or ELSE.

Bill and I crawled into the rig, with me behind the wheel. We stared at each other—neither of us ever had any experience with one of these giants. Bill just looked at me and said this must be it—goodbye! At that very moment we both noticed a plaque above the windshield in the center portion which gave shifting instructions. The remaining problem was how to start. We finally figured that out as the lieutenant was beginning to lose patience with us.

When we moved a few feet, he yelled something at us, and then all his men, including himself, jumped into the truck. Then we took off, following sign directions the officer was giving us through the rear view window. In the meantime, Bill and I began to breathe again. When we arrived at a camp site that they'd set up, they all jumped out of the truck, and the lieutenant told us what to do. We were handed two old rags and told to dust off this big rig—one that had been running over dusty roads for months. By now, it was getting near supper time, and Bill and I were quite hungry. During all those past days we spent in the jungle we had eaten only greens which Sgt. Calm knew to be safe, and also some wild berries.

As soon as we finished dusting off the truck, the lieutenant came over to inspect our work. He apparently was satisfied by what he saw, but insisted we open the hood. We thought maybe he wanted us to check oil or something. When we finally figured out how to open the lid, he looked in at the motor and began screaming something. It was obvious he was furious at us because we both got knocked to the ground. We knew then that we were also supposed to dust off the motor. It was quite a job, but once we finished, he was finally satisfied and ordered two rice balls to be brought to us. We devoured them in less than a minute. We were then told to sleep on the ground. During the night, whenever we fell asleep, a guard would come along, prod us with his bayonet and flash a light in our face—then satisfied he would walk off. Orders or pure sadism.

In the morning we were given another small curried rice ball. After this we all got into the truck and were directed where to go. They had us drive on trails that were almost impossible. Somehow—I'll never know how—we made it. Finally, when we reached an ammunition and artillery site, they loaded the military arms and ammunition on the truck. The next problem was trying to turn this huge truck around. It was no easy job and was always dangerous. We knew we dare not fail, as that would be signing our death warrant. This little endurance test continued for about five or six days. Every day we were forced to dust off our truck upon returning.

As we drove the truck along the roads, we suddenly realized we'd been passing some of the men from our unit. They were walking along the road dressed in civilian clothes. Whenever they recognized us they'd give us a high sign. Then we'd honk the horn. That decision the men had made back in our camp to head out on their own seemed, at this stage, to have been a wise one. These were really very emotional moments for all of us.

Then one morning the Japanese Lieutenant came to us carrying two little bags of rice. First he took away the truck. Then he made us understand that we were to head for Bagac and then walk across Bataan to Balanga. We tried to prevail on him for a ride part way, but no luck. He told us to get going. So off Bill and I trudged, each carrying our small bag of rice. We reached Bagac and turned to head across Bataan. As we did so, every so often we would come across a road sentry. It was the same every time—stop and get searched for goodies and then pushed on. A very strange thing happened as we crossed. One sentry, after searching us, would chase us on, but the next one would actually give us each a cigarette before motioning us to move along. We couldn't figure it out. The days were exhausting and at night we would sleep alongside the road. We were lonely and frightened all the time, as no traffic whatsoever ever went by, not even during daylight.

Chapter 7

The First POW Gathering Place

"We who lived in concentration camps can remember the men who walked through, comforting others, giving away their last bit of food. They may have been few in number, but they offer sufficient proof that everything can be taken from a man but one thing; the last of human freedoms—to choose one's attitude in any given set of circumstances—to choose one's own way."

Viktor Frankl

hort of Balanga, although we did not know exactly how far, we came across this guarded camp. We guessed we were to stay there until further orders. We knew nothing as to what was coming next and were filled with dread. This little area had about seventy-five to a hundred POW's in it. The next morning, a POW came rushing over to us. He had seen our Red Cross arm bands and asked if we were doctors. He told us one of the men was in terrible shape and asked if we could do something to help him. We went over and examined the young man. He, indeed, was in agonizing pain, and we both agreed he was having a severe case of acute appendicitis. We told him he needed surgery, but had nothing that we could use. He begged us to do anything at all—he was ready for anything and, if we couldn't, he begged us to help him die quickly. Bill and I put our heads together and asked others there to find some pieces of glass. If a piece was suitable, I would use it to cut. At the same time, one of them brought a spool of brown sewing thread and a small needle. I told the sick man we could possibly get the appendix out with what had been found. I was troubled because it was dangerous at best. If the appendix ruptured, he would quite surely die. Surgery would be taking a chance—painful beyond belief, as we had no anesthetic. Did he want to take this risk? It was his choice. He told us to go ahead and do whatever we could. If he was going to die anyway, he wanted to go with a fighting chance. Believe me, this was all pretty hard for Bill and I to take. We boiled the glass, thread and needle, and I proceeded to cut down. Men were holding him down, but, surprisingly, although he yelled, he did not struggle too much. I controlled the bleeding with thread and needle and finally entered the abdomen. The appendix was ready to rupture—it was gangrenous. I removed it and proceeded to close the incision, which was difficult because of the irregular incision made with the sharp piece of glass. I was wringing wet when I finished—no bandage, just a piece of cloth from clothes, the same unsterilized cloth I had to use pieces of as a sponge. Even though I told him the dangers of infection when I finished, he almost made me burst into tears and my heart must have skipped a beat with words I never have forgotten. "Thanks, Doc, you did your best, and may God take care of you." I fumbled for words and told him I hoped God would take care of him. What a brave young man and what a spirit! It was strange that very few of the POW's stood around us as we worked. They seemed to understand the nature of these weird proceedings. If it wasn't that, it may have been that they were too sick and/or exhausted to watch.

For the days following I watched him carefully, and although the cut area was quite red, there didn't seem to be any severe infection setting in. Every time I walked away from him, I said a prayer—this courageous young man deserved a chance at life.

Finally, the day came when Bill and I were forced to leave and march to Balanga along with others. The patient remained behind but appeared to be doing OK and even walked a bit. I never saw him again, but later on, many months later, one of the prisoners walked up to me and said, "Remember the soldier whose appendix you took out?" I almost fell over when he said the young man wanted me to know he was doing well and was able to continue on the death march. The irony of it got to me. At this time I felt like the Big Man upstairs was looking over our shoulders and was responsible for this young man's recovery. What a wonderful feeling it was, and how grateful I felt! As I thought about this years later, I wondered if my compassion had got the best of my sane judgment. It was a consolation to know he'd recovered. Although what I did seemed like a crazy long shot, it was at least better than just standing saying, "There's nothing to be done."

We finally reached the camp at Balanga, a barbed wire enclosure filled with POW's. Bill and I had just a little rice left. One of the men saw it and wanted it so badly that he said he would trade us a little salt for it. Men were dropping by the road and we thought that because of loss of salt in perspiration this would be a good deal, so we traded. The death march was in no way over, and this salt would come in handy.

It had taken just about a half day marching to reach

this camp. The enclosure was packed with men who had already been on the grueling death march from Mariveles and other spots to the south. Where we would eventually go was anybody's guess. Men were already sick—deadly sick from malnutrition, dysentery, malaria and other conditions. There were no latrines—defecation and urination were done where anyone could find an open space of ground. I have no words to really describe the filthy conditions that existed. We had begun to despair.

We were still wearing our arm bands. When the war began, we'd been told to wear them, but because we were non-combatants, we didn't carry side arms. As the war progressed, the Japanese snipers took delight in picking on officers, so we were told to take off all insignia. Since they were also often shooting at us, we'd then been told that we could wear side arms for our own protection. Of course, after the surrender no one wore side arms, but some of us carried on with our arm bands.

The camp was a mess. We slept on the ground and were lucky if we weren't right on top of human waste. Conditions were so bad that at times we only hoped they would march us soon to some place, any place, just to get out of the hell hole. While there I heard some very sad news about Dr. Warshell. After he had turned himself in at Mariveles, the Japanese had the prisoners line up. They were to have the usual inspection, which the Japanese loved to carry out, confiscating the usual valuables. Arnold, I remember, somehow was able to obtain a Japanese wrist watch from one of our front line patients. He wore it all the time, obviously obsessed with his souvenir. Apparently he had forgotten to take it off when he turned himself in. In the course of the search of men who were lined up, the officer came to him and immediately spotted the watch. Arnold was knocked to the ground, and soldiers were ordered to take him into the woods. Shots were heard—the soldiers returned, but no Arnold.

Dr. Pizer and Dr. Waters, I am told, made it through the death march, and were able eventually to return to the United States.

One day an interpreter saw my arm band and came up to me. After asking if I was a medical officer, he said, "Follow me." While this was going on, the Japanese were taking men from the crowd and lining them up as if a parade was to begin. Each line had five abreast—I don't recall how many rows. The interpreter took me to the front of the line and said, "You are the leader. You have two hundred men behind you. When the march is over, be sure you have these two hundred men or you will pay with your life." Panicked, I tried to explain that I would have no way of preventing illness, exhaustion, or men falling out for assorted reasons. Sadly, I got nowhere with him.

I walked from the front of the line to the rear, cautioning all the men to try their best not to fall out as the consequences might be severe. Maybe I was thinking of my own hide at that time. Each man was given one rice ball and a canteen of water.

As we walked out, I could only think of the terrible condition most of the men were in. Some even had trouble standing, much less trying to walk. We were under heavy guard and the guards were tough looking. We'd marched only a few blocks when the first man collapsed. His fellow POW's tried to hold him up, but it was impossible. When he fell at the roadside, one of the guards put a bullet into his head. As a result many thought "Why even try? We might as well quit now and accept our fate." Yet there were others who would yell to keep going at all costs.

We were marched in the heat of the day in temperatures well up to and over 100 degrees. Our energy gave out and also our will to carry on. We were thirsty, perspiring, hungry, and exhausted, even at the start.

As evening descended, we were herded into a sort of collecting area where we would spend the night. No latrines—no more food. As before, you relieved yourself where you stood or where you were lying. The odor was nauseating and dysentery was even getting to the more healthy men.

These were the conditions we had to endure for the remainder of the death march, which took about seven days.

The march finally ended near the town of San Fernando, where we were walked into a guarded compound greeted by more guards. At any moment I expected a roll call and count. I knew that of my own group of two hundred, I had lost about eight men. They died of exhaustion and dehydration faster than from starvation. I remembered a sad incident during the march. A man walking directly behind me started yelling for water. At the exact time we were passing a well in which water was flowing out to irrigate the farmer's sugar cane. The man lost control and dashed out for a drink. As he bent over and turned his head up, so as to have the water hit his mouth, a guard was watching him. At that very moment the guard took aim and hit him in the head. He fell into the water and lay there as the guard walked up and pumped a few more bullets into him. When the guard walked away to join the column as though nothing had happened, we all began to realize what was going to lie ahead for us wherever we might be taken. Our enemies

Death March

obviously hated us, especially for surrendering.

We stood there and waited while the guards were looking us over. Although no count was made then, I could only think of what would happen to me when they did count. Finally, one guard came over and motioned me to have the men fall out. I took a deep breath and thanked the Big Man upstairs as I realized the threat to me had not been forgotten. When I was allowed to dismiss the men, some scattered among the other prisoners. Others just lay down where they were standing, totally beat physically. So many came to me asking if I could help them with assorted medical problems, but my answer was always the same. I had no medicines, no instruments, nothing. It was a truly helpless feeling. The death march from Mariveles to this point had been about sixty-five miles and from where we started had to be at least fifty miles.

As I surveyed the camp, I felt deep sorrow. Sick and exhausted men lay all over, trying their best to control their problems. There were no sanitary facilities here either. As I looked about, I thought these men must be endowed with superhuman power to keep trying to carry on. The will to live was obvious.

As I stood in amazement, a guard came up to me and grabbed me by the arm, motioning me to follow him. In terror of being finished off because I didn't have the entire two hundred men on arrival, I thought this was to be the end. He took me to a fence, at the rear of a guard station. As we stood there, another guard on the other side of the fence came over and handed him two eggs. They talked in Japanese for a while. Then the other guard left. At that point the first guard turned to me and handed me one egg. I held it as he took the other one, cracked the end open and sucked out the contents. He motioned me to do likewise. Was this to be the Last Supper?

The guard then gestured to me to return to my men and disappeared as quickly as he had approached. Perhaps the egg was poisoned. My fright was irrational. The egg had been intact. Why had he singled me out for that momentary treat? After all, I was just another prisoner. I never learned the reason but sure was grateful.

There was one rather large bonfire in the camp and I knew the wood ashes might help dysentery which was causing so much suffering. When I told some of the men to eat the cooled ashes, word got around, since ash was medicinal, the men were scrambling to get it as fast as their condition permitted. Pitiful, to say the least. As time went on, and the fire gradually burned itself out, there was not a teaspoonful of ash left.

One morning a contingent of men were selected and lined up. I was one of them. We were led to a railroad station where a freight train was standing, its doors wide open. As they motioned us to pile into the cars, the Japanese seemed to be counting how many men were in each car. They packed us in so tight that we could only fit standing up. Then, with a count of a hundred men to a car, the doors were slammed shut. As we were piled in, at first we all thought: "at least we're going to get a train ride to some destination." Soon, with no ventilation, we realized we were in for another ordeal. Men could only relieve themselves where they stood. Though the stench was hard to take, there was no alternative and very little grumbling. Along with the smell, the heat was unbearable. Many of the men just collapsed, which only made matters worse. Since there was no place for a man to fall, some were held up by the sheer crowded condition of the car.

After a ride that seemed to go on forever, we finally stopped. When the doors were flung open, everyone literally fell out. Suddenly there was fresh air—a treasured gift from Heaven. What a treat just to breathe it in.

We were told we were now at Capas. It turned out that this station was a short distance from our destination— Camp O'Donnell, a camp that had been developed by General MacArthur some time before the war broke out. I'd been told it was his intention to give better training to the Philippine Army, but war had broken out before any training could be given there.

As soon as we were led to this camp, we were lined up to get the usual speech by the Japanese Commander. He reminded us of our disgrace in surrendering and warned us to obey all camp regulations.

Camp O'Donnell was made of Nipa shacks, most without flooring, all of which were located on a hill. From this site we could look down the hill. At a distance of two or so miles we could see the camp where all the Filipino soldiers were located. Their death toll was very high—all day long there was a constant line of men carrying their dead to the mass burial grounds. I had expected a terrible death toll, but at the Filipino camp the death rate was around three hundred daily. In our camp we were losing fifty to a hundred men every day. At least we were finally in a place that had a few water wells. The demand for water was so great and the line so long that I sometimes gave up. Of course, everyone needed water, so the lines even continued after dark. Once a day we were served a small ball of rice, and occasionally a little curry.

Finally, our POW hospital was established. Unfortunately, at first it was a hospital in name only since we doctors had no medicine. The best we did then was give moral support and recommend eating ashes to help control the dysentery. By a twist of fate the Japanese requested a work detail to be taken out of camp under guard and to perform whatever was requested. While out on these details the men somehow made contacts with the civilians. After a while we asked them to bring in guava leaves, knowing that if they were made into a tea, it could also help control the diarrhea that was raging through the camp. Some smuggled them in and others arranged to have them placed near our fence during the night. In the morning the men would go to the designated place and pick them up. Without these leaves, left by compassionate civilians, we would have lost even more men.

Even today, when I think of our hospital, I feel much pain. We had literally nothing to treat sickness or injury. The very ill hardly ever came out of it, except feet first and carried to our mass burial ground.

It was here that I met Dr. Herbst, who'd been an internist in private practice in Canton, Ohio before he entered service. And it was here that I finally had the courage to try to help medically, despite the lack of... well, everything!

Chapter 8

Camp Cabanatuan

"History never looks like history when you are living through it. It always looks confusing and messy, and it always feels uncomfortable."

John Gardner

Sometime in June, 1942 we were placed in trucks and taken to camp 1 at Cabanatuan. There were three sections in this area. Dr. Herbst, a few corpsmen, and I were appointed to section one, where we established what was to be called a first aid station. Sadly, it was also one that operated without medicine or instruments. At first this made it a great place to come with medical problems as long as you didn't expect to get anything but sympathy. Our barracks was located on the corner nearest the road. The senior officer section was on the far side with the rest of the men were in between. The food in this camp consisted of rice, nothing else. Eventually work details were taken to a river and the greens in the river were brought back to camp for us to eat along with rice. I know for sure that without those greens none of us would have survived.

Although still without instruments, I found a few pieces of broken glass and used them to incise and drain abscesses along with other surgical procedures. It was around this time that I decided that even without proper equipment I was going to somehow manage to function as a doctor again.

An interesting piece of life saving deceit was carried out in our camp. This POW I shall refer to as WERM somehow managed to smuggle sulfa tablets into camp. He also managed to contact a Japanese guard, making a deal to trade a few of the sulfa tablets for some extra food. The Japanese wanted this medication very much in order to treat their gonorrhea. Many had gotten gonorrhea from rape rather than relationships—vicious attacks on civilian women who were innocently infected with it.

WERM did not share this extra food generally—only with his close friends and buddies. When the demand for more sulfa finally exceeded the supply, he had to come up with a substitute. Somehow he managed to get his hand on baking soda, and made careful molds so the end product would look exactly like the real tablet. This was Werm's version of the "sulfa tablet." In spite of the tablets being fake and the Japanese soldiers taking a fake tablet, they kept on asking for more. I guess if our enemies had ever found out that they were being duped, he would have been a dead man. They didn't find out and, as I learned years later, he made it through the entire ordeal and returned home.

Chapter 9
The Tatori Maru

"Experience is the worst teacher—it gives the test
before presenting the lesson."

Vernon Law

On October 8, 1942 a detail of 1500 men was
selected to be taken to Manila. At that time, no
one knew the destination. I was selected to go
with them as the surgeon with Dr. Herbst as internist. A
Dr. Mosiman, who was in the camp, was also selected.

One of the senior officers went to Japanese headquarters to plead for me to stay behind because I was a surgeon. He asked them to send some other doctors, as I was
so needed at the camp. The Japanese Commandant was
adamant and said, "He goes."

We were taken to Manila to what I believe were the
remains of Pier 7. The other docks had been shot up and
bombed pretty thoroughly. Inside we all sat or lay around,
trying to get something to eat and drink. Alongside the
dock a Japanese freighter was tied up. We somehow
found out that it had come from the South Seas.
Somewhere down there, it had been hit by a shell or torpedo near its propeller. Its main shaft was slightly out of
line and could go only very slowly. The ship also had car-

ried a contingent of enemy soldiers from the south. They lived in one of the holds while being transported. This ship was the Tatori Maru, the first POW ship to carry prisoners northward. Although some of us wondered why us and where were we going, the detail really turned out to be a blessing in disguise. Some ships that left later were attacked and sunk by American forces. No ships were marked POW, so it was obvious why they would be attacked. Many men were lost as a consequence of these attacks.

We were all told to board ship, our men to go into the remaining holds. Aboard deck was an open trough-like wooden latrine hung and emptied over the side of the ship. Alongside was a barrel like container supposedly for defecation. The trough was used for both defecation and urination, providing the men in the holds could get there in time. Many still suffered from dysentery, so most of the time men could not make it to the trough. As a result, it wasn't long before the holds really stank. All the going and coming was closely watched by the guards, so that no loitering would occur.

Only eighteen men were allowed to sleep on deck. I was one of the fortunate ones since after leaving the port of Manila, we had constant fresh air. Further north the winds became cold and all of us wore only tropical fatigues. Treatment for the sick consisted of moral support, which was all we could give since we had nothing. We also found out that the ship was not marked as a POW transport. This made us sitting ducks for the American Naval Forces.

When we left Manila, we were part of an escorted convoy but since we weren't able to maintain the same speed as the convoy, we were soon left behind to proceed on our own. Pretty scary. When we were north of the Lingayen gulf, our fears became reality. Suddenly the ship siren and whistle sounded. Simultaneously, the ship began to make sharp turns. The men on deck spotted the wake of two torpedoes and cried out. There was general panic as those who were able began to crawl out of the holds. Some even wanted to jump into the water. At the same time all the guards who had been on the deck suddenly disappeared, as if by magic. Luckily, the skipper of the ship maneuvered it so cleverly that both torpedoes missed us, one passing on either side. We were afraid another might be on its way. We stood in silence and watched until our eyes were bulging out, but luckily nothing further happened. The skipper headed towards our destination, at the same time another signal sounded which we presumed to be the all clear.

After this scare there was a run on the so-called latrines. The guards suddenly appeared from nowhere.

Heading northward, land was spotted ahead of us. As we approached, we saw what appeared to be an inlet and port. Turning into it and proceeding slowly to dock, we found out that we were at the port city of Takao on the island of Taiwan, which in those days was known as Formosa. After standing there for some time, a board like plank was lowered from the ship to the dock. On the dock were lots of hoses with running salt water. As soon as we were told that the men could go on the dock and clean up with the hose water, most of them left the ship, took their clothes off and watered down with a great sigh of joy.

One man who was coming down the plank slipped and fell to the dock. I was called over to see him and determined that he had broken his upper arm rather badly.

The question was how to immobilize it and with what? I had men scatter around on the dock. Finally one man found a broken wooden fruit box that I could break up further to make a splint. Another man came up with some pieces of canvas. I figured I could tear it up with strips to use in immobilization. Pieces of it could be used for a little padding on the wooden slab. By sheer touch and by manipulation I tried my best to get the fragments in a relatively good position. As I was doing this, it was not very comfortable for the patient! At times he would cry out. I finally proceeded to immobilize his arm with my home made splint. With the procedure finished he boarded the ship again with some help.

After we were ordered to board ship there was another wait. Later we headed out to sea, turning northward. We came upon a small island where we dropped anchor and stayed for several days. The rumor was that we were awaiting an all clear signal to proceed, due to some submarine activity to the north.

Life was not being exactly kind—after the awaited signal was received we left again. As we sped northward, we ran into extremely heavy winds and cold rain. A tropical monsoon had hit—the winds were unbelievable. I had to tie myself to a section of the ship to keep from getting washed overboard. The waves were like mountains. We began to wonder just how much beating could this old freighter, made in Scotland in 1868, take.

As we were heading northward, eighteen of our men died. They were brought to the deck, a prayer was said, and as we stood at attention, they were slid off a board into the ocean. Because of the freezing wind many other men began to get upper respiratory infections, and some, I am sure, had pneumonia. But how could I be sure with-

out any stethoscope? No medicine, no instruments. What
to do? It was depressing to admit that up to this point my
POW life had a main theme song: "Sorry, we have no
medicine." A few times I had ignored the lack of suitable
instruments and antibiotics to "go in" anyhow and somehow—even if I had to use a piece of broken glass, do
what had to be done surgically to save the patient. But
the method was frightening. Had I just been lucky?

Chapter 10

Land Again—Korea and Manchuria

"You can discover what your enemy fears most by observing the means he uses to frighten you."

Eric Hoffer

W e finally docked at a port, which we found out was Fusan, Korea, later called Pusan. Approximately twelve hundred men were taken off. The rest of them were to go on—to where we were not told. At Fusan approximately three hundred to five hundred men were to remain, and Dr. Mosiman was to stay with them. These men were considered the most seriously ill, and probably not capable of going on further. All of us were given warmer Chinese clothes when we left. It was hard to say goodbye to Dr. Mosiman and his sick men.

Then we were paraded through the streets of the city to the utter amazement of the civilians, who watched us go by. When we arrived at a railroad station we were herded into passenger cars and were joined by a contingent of some six hundred British officers and men. Can you imagine our surprise? Were we in Heaven? Passenger cars, not freight cars. We finally knew we were indeed in Heaven when the guards came through the cars and handed out boxes of lunch. Inside we found rice, fish, and, best of all, a small tangerine. We were looking at a great feast. We almost didn't want to eat it because it would be gone. Hungry as we were, we ate it very slowly, savoring every mouthful. Up to now, all us American prisoners traveled with no other clothing. We were amazed to see the British wearing woolen clothes and carrying knapsacks with extra woolens.

As pleased as we all were, there seemed to be an air of suspicion in most of us. Knowing how the Japanese had been so very clever and that kindness to us was not one of their usual traits, we began to wonder if we were not being treated so nicely because ahead, wherever we were being taken, would come the ultimate surprise.

The train took us to Mukden, Manchuria, a city of some million or more people. In previous years it had been called Hoten, before the enemy overran it. We departed from the train and were lined up and marched to a camp with barbed wire fences and guard towers. The barracks inside were made of slats of wood, and the roof of clay and weeds. They were sunk about two feet into the ground and the remainder of the barracks were above ground level. Inside the barracks were long bunks on each side of the wall. In the center was a Russian type stove called a Pietchka. The bunks were little straw covered mattresses and each had four to six military blankets. No sheets of course. While inside, we noticed that some of the clay had fallen away from between the boarding so that in areas you could see daylight. That meant we had to hunt around and find whatever was available to plug these cracks and keep the cold winds from blowing through them.

Before we were dismissed to go to these barracks, we

had to stand and wait for the Japanese Camp Commander, Colonel Matsuyama, to give us the usual "Bushido" lecture. After we stood waiting in freezing weather, he finally came out and we heard the old story. Remember that it was now November 11, 1942, and the cold winds blowing off the Gobi desert made the wind chill feel even colder. We were dismissed and directed to our respective barracks. The officers' quarters were closest to enemy headquarters. One-half of the officers' barracks were assigned to the American officers, the other half to the British officers.

The camp had two interpreters—both enlisted men. One was Kawashima, a private and former resident of Hawaii. He was quite sympathetic to us without making it too obvious to the other Japanese. He helped when he could without overstepping sound judgment. The other interpreter was Corporal Noda. He'd been a resident of Berkeley, California, where he attended school but had returned to Japan before the outbreak of war to resume his studies. When war broke out, he'd been conscripted into the interpreters' service. He was the opposite of Kawashima, hating every one of us and taking every opportunity to make our lives miserable. At the time of the war crimes trial, after the Japanese surrender, he was sentenced to twenty years and only served seven. He should have received the death sentence.

At the beginning, one of the barracks was assigned to be the hospital, where people on sick call could be held. Again, this so-called hospital was no different than any of the other barracks, even to the same kind of mattresses and bunks.

Each barracks was given one bucket of coal per day, which could not be used until 4:00 in the afternoon.

Within a couple of days we were called into the headquarters as the Commandant wanted to discuss our
future rations. Up to then we had only rice. Hankins, the
ranking officer, Dr. Herbst, Arnold Bocksell and I participated in the talks. We were told that we could have soy
beans in place of rice. Great news. We knew the beans are
rich in protein, while rice is mainly a carbohydrate. We
didn't need much carbohydrate. What our bodies needed
most at that time would be protein. Arnold also heavily
promoted the idea of corn meal. The Commandant acted
very pleased and assured us we would get both. We were
given small amounts of barley at times. In later years, I
found out that rice was a scarce and precious commodity
in Japan. They were having big problems in bringing it up
from Southeast Asia, as their farmers could not produce
enough in Japan to cover their needs.

The next day some trucks pulled into camp, and the
beans and some corn meal were unloaded. Every man in
the camp gladly offered to unload the trucks, ecstatic to
know we would have beans.

The same day, while in the hospital barracks, Dr.
Herbst and I were introduced to the Japanese doctor,
Capt. Kawajima, who was assigned to the camp. Through
the interpreter we were given instructions as to what he
expected of us. We could admit a man, but he would
remain only if the Japanese doctor put his final OK on
the admission. If we needed a drug, he would decide
whether it was necessary and the dose to be given. He
would try and see all our patients every day, and we could
not get any medicine unless he ordered it.

This camp became what I understood to be designated
as Camp Hoten. It had originally served as Chinese
Cavalry Cantonment camp. Besides the barracks for

POW's, we had a storehouse for food and a barracks for cooking. The latrines were of the same construction and had two troughs and some stalls for defecation. In the cook house were a couple of ovens made of brick and also cauldrons in which cooking could be done.

When the cooks made soy beans at the start, they prepared them in the usual manner in which beans are cooked. Everyone was anxious to get them. We quickly found out that the beans were rather rubbery and hard to chew. So what? We swallowed them anyway. Then the surprises came. When any of us had a bowel movement, the beans would fly out as if shot from a gun. This continued for several days. No one was sure why they were so indigestible. The chief cook was a Polish chap, a sergeant named Andy. He decided on a new way to cook the beans. He would start them in the evening, cook them all night to be served the next day, maybe 24 hours later. This turned out to be the answer. They were digestible, and everyone enjoyed them. The corn meal was made into either a mush or a bread similar to what we call corn meal bread.

Back to the hospital. When the Japanese doctor did dole out any medication, he acted like he was paying for it. Of course, I am sure that the pharmacy where he got the drugs had very little to begin with. For example, when quinine was requested, we received half the dose we usually used.

One day, in making rounds with the doctor, I told him a certain patient had pneumonia, and I needed medication. He said no and, using sign language, indicated that I should remove some blood from the patient's arm and inject it into the patient's buttocks. He also indicated that this manner of treatment was used very successfully by the Japanese. I told him I was very sorry and refused to follow his instructions. I said American doctors did not treat pneumonias with this kind of autoinoculation.

The next moment I found myself lying on the floor. He struck me on the side of my head with the flat of his hand. I got up and looked him straight in the eye, as if as to say "doctors don't act that way." However, he repeated his order and left. In a short period of time, a Japanese corps man appeared carrying a syringe and alcohol sponge and handed it to me. He stood over me to watch and see if I would do it. I had no alternative but to carry out the procedure. I couldn't believe that they as professionals could be so inhuman. Two days later the poor chap died.

About this time I was seeing certain cases that I realized would need surgery immediately or later. Our hospital barracks, of course, had no equipment or medicine. The thought occurred to me, that in Mukden the Japanese must have some type of hospital to handle the medical needs of their soldiers. I took a chance and asked for permission to talk to the Camp Commandant about this problem to see if there was any possibility of getting patients to their hospital. After being granted the interview I was sure this whole conference was useless. Up to then, no matter where we were, it seemed like they couldn't care less if one of us lived or died. By their thinking, if one died, it would be one less to feed.

The Commandant seemed interested and asked many questions as to who would go and who was the surgeon. When we were finished, I left. I finally realized that I must have been dreaming to even think of such a possibility much less having it become a reality. The days went by and we did our work in the camp as usual. Then one day I was called to Headquarters.

The Commandant told me they had arranged to give me a thirty bed ward in the Imperial Army Hospital in Mukden. The patients who might be considered to go there would have to be approved by the Camp Japanese doctor and that only I would go.

I was to be ready to leave early in the morning to go with the camp truck. Patients would also have to go on the truck—no ambulance. I would be taken to the Japanese dentist's office every morning where I would then have to do whatever had to be done. Then I'd report back to the dentist's office where I was to wait for the truck and guards to take me back to camp. I was told the truck would never return to camp until late afternoon or early evening, depending on how fast they accomplished their own duties. I couldn't believe my ears. Were they starting to become compassionate? Yet, I began to wonder what was I getting myself into. If something heavy happened at the hospital, would I be held accountable?

Potential problems began to float through my head. Yes, I would be working at times in the hospital. Yet, I knew no Japanese and was not familiar with any of their medicines. On top of that, I knew that the Japanese used drugs at one-half the dose we usually gave to our men under similar conditions. These thoughts swirled through my head. However, I still had a feeling that maybe I could do some good for our men if they needed it. So all I could say, to myself, was that time would tell what I got myself into.

The following morning I left with the guards and rode on the open portion of the truck. Believe me, it was bitter cold out there. Three soldiers rode in the cab. In the one corner of the truck, just back of the cab, was a charcoal

burner which had been fired up. It was this that was used
for fuel. Obviously, gas was a scarce commodity. I hud-
dled as close as I could to this burner to gather a little
heat. I had no idea where or how far we were going, and
prayed that it wouldn't be too far away. We finally arrived
at a very pretentious red brick building. It was quite large
and left me totally surprised. The guard took me in and
led me to the dentist's office where I was told by the dentist, who spoke some English, that when I would be
dropped off in the morning, I was to come to this
office—the guards would not come in with me. In the
evening the guard would let me know they were ready to
return.

Oddly, the Japanese dentist and I seemed to strike
some degree of compatibility. Through his very broken
English I found out that he'd been a civilian who was
called into service and attached to this hospital. As time
went on, we got along very well. I found out that he studied dentistry at a school in Kansas. He told me he hadn't
spoken English for many years since leaving the States. I
was surprised to find out how much he really retained. It
was remarkable. On my first trips he took me around the
hospital and made me acquainted with the various
departments, including the place where I would have the
surgical beds.

Chapter 11

The First Surgical Case

"History is a pact between the dead, the living,
and the yet unborn."

Edmund Burke

t wasn't much longer when a POW showed up choking for lack of air. After examining him, I felt he had an infected thyroglossal cyst obstructing his airway. It is a cyst lying low in the back of the throat and tongue. I remember having seen only one when I was in private practice. I called the Japanese doctor and explained the situation. It should have been obvious to him or anyone for that matter that this man was in a dire state.

He agreed and arrangements were made to take the patient to the hospital. The trip in the open truck was an ordeal for him. He needed a tracheotomy but that was not possible. A Japanese doctor agreed to the surgery. They prepared the operating room and necessary help. A Japanese doctor came to me and informed me in sign language that he was going to assist me. I was grateful for that because he could lead me through their preparations.

I followed him into a large room where a large table stood in the center. There were two piles of white clothing on either side of the table. He went to one side and motioned me to the other. I gathered that the clothing in front of us were gowns. I decided I would watch him and do exactly what he would.

He stripped down to his bare skin, so I did likewise. He then put one of his gowns on. I was taken back that they did not use OR suits. Anyway, I put on my gown, but, wow, it was short! I guess that is because as a rule the Japanese were shorter than us. When I looked at myself, I realized that mine extended only down to about my pubic bone. What showed below was what we refer to as the "family jewels." I was a bit embarrassed, but I had a job to do.

We went into a scrub room, and he and I began our scrub. It seems like my short gown and the display below was creating an unusually interesting display for the nurses and OR assistants. I say this because of the extraordinary number of nurses who seemed to go through the room, glance at me, and then walk out giggling. I guess you could refer to this as the first American display in Manchuria. When we finished, he led the way into the operating room. Wow! It was filled wall to wall with what I presume were doctors and nurses. There must have been at least thirty to forty in the room. I guess word had gotten around that the American surgeon was going to operate and evidently they wanted to see how we worked.

We slipped on sterile gowns and then, instead of rubber gloves, we were given white cotton gloves, similar to the kind morticians give pall bearers in this country. I was dumbfounded. I found out much later that the Japanese used those gloves instead of rubber because of the difficulty they were having in getting rubber up from Southeast Asia. The doctor at the head of the table somehow managed to put the patient to sleep. I didn't know with what, and never did find out. Starting the operation, I soon found out that I had a serious problem. I had trouble feeling instruments properly through those cotton gloves and had considerable trouble trying to tie knots. Not wanting to make a fool out of myself or American surgery, I decided to take the gloves off, and threw them on the floor.

As I did that, there was considerable mumbling in the room and Japanese talk increased. I can only guess they must have been saying something like, "Look at the crazy American. He is going to operate with his bare hands."

The diagnosis proved correct, and I was able to drain the infected cyst and alleviate the problem. I closed up with drains in place and left the OR as they took the patient to the ward. As I reflect on this episode, I often wondered why they seemed to want to help—both before, during and after the surgery. Judging from my previous experiences on the death march and later, it was so uncharacteristic of them.

I saw the patient and left instructions as to his care before leaving for the dentist's office. Word had spread quickly even to him. He said he'd heard I did a great job. Boy, they sure had a good underground system in the hospital to spread word around as to what is going on. Since it was not time for my guard, he took me into his laboratory and fed me a little rice and a piece of fish he had probably saved from his rations.

As I got to know him better, at mealtime if I was there, he would send the nurses out of his office, telling them to return at a certain time. Then we'd go into the lab. Door closed, he would share a little of his food with me. In reality we were enemies, yet here was a man who must have understood our predicament and shared what he could with me. I guess it sort of finally sealed a bond between us. I don't know why we struck it off. I always felt he had a soft spot in his heart for Americans, but never dared show it to others or he would have paid the supreme penalty.

One more interesting thing happened while we were in the room putting on our gowns. After he'd put on his, he proceeded to remove his shoes and stockings. This was another new one for me. I did the same, and then I noticed he slipped into a pair of "Getas," which were under the table. This is a wooden flat slipper with two cross bands of cloth that you slip between your big and second toe. When I slipped into mine, I realized that my heels hung over the back by about one inch, more or less. Here, again, the Japanese had smaller feet, and we had bigger ones. It was uncomfortable, to say the least.

While I waited in his office for the guard to show up, the dentist took care of his patients. I had trouble trying to understand why in all my trips both into and out of camp I was never searched. I was probably the only POW to ever leave and return to a Japanese POW camp and never get searched. Many times on the way back to camp the truck would make a stop and leave me alone in it. Why? Who was I? Did they just trust me? On one trip back, they stopped at what I am sure was a Geisha house and all went in. I sat alone in the dark and bitter cold. Few people were on the street. Finally, after about an hour, they came out, pretty jovial.

When I say "cold," I really mean freezing. In the winter, when the winds blew out of the Gobi desert, the temperature would at times fall to forty degrees below zero, and when snow fell, not very often, it would fall horizon-

tally rather than vertically. The Gobi winds were responsible for that. In spite of frequent bouts of shivering, I
had to be careful and never complain, for fear any com-
plaint might jeopardize the surgical project.

In due time, I found out that this hospital was one of
two in Manchuria serving the Kwantung Army. The
other, I am told, was in Harbin. The Kwawntung Army
was made up of mainly Manchurians, who were mostly
larger than the Japanese but were led by Japanese officers
and non-commissioned officers.

Chapter 12

An Escape

"Until the day of his death no man can be sure of his courage."

Jean Anouilh

I *recall a rather sad event* that happened in the camp. One day we had an unexpected body count. It developed that we were three men short—they had managed to escape. The new Camp Commandant, a Colonel Matsuda, was furious and let us feel his rage. I worried that maybe he would toughen up and discontinue the surgical hospital program. Instead he established a rule of ten. Men were counted in groups of ten, and each one in the ten was to be responsible for the others. If one escaped, the new rule was that all the remaining nine would be held guilty and suffer the death penalty.

Some days later, we were told that the elite military police of the Japanese had caught the three escapees in a Manchurian province some distance from camp. They had approached a Manchurian farmer for some food. Supposedly he informed the military police post, but in the course of events the farmer was killed. Further, we were told that they were tried and found guilty of com-

mitting murder, and were sentenced to death. My understanding was that they were three Marines. They were
shot and the bodies were given to us for burial. At the
burial site we discovered it was close to a Chinese burial
place. We could see mounds which held the dead in
which objects had been placed to accompany the
deceased. Needless to say, this burial was an unhappy
event.

Chapter 13
The New Mukden Camp

"Experience is not what happens to a man. It is
what a man does with what's happened to him."

Aldous Huxley

One day we were told we were being transferred to
a new camp. We were loaded into trucks in July,
1943 and taken to the other side of Mukden.
This camp had a brick wall around it, with barbed wire
on top. We never knew whether the wire had electric cur-
rent or not, and no one seemed willing to try and find
out. The many buildings inside the wall consisted of three
large barracks two stories high, a mess hall, or rather a
cook shop, a supposed "recreation" building, a two story
questionable hospital building, a bath and powerhouse-
like building, and at one end of the enclosure several
buildings which housed the Japanese soldiers and their
headquarters.

The American and British POW's each had separate
buildings. At that time we had about a thousand
Americans, and at one time there were about six hundred
British. In the first year we lost approximately two hundred men, but managed somehow to cut that down so
that in the last year we lost only about fifteen.

Our camp eventually held POW's of all ranks from the United States, Great Britain New Zealand, Australia, and Holland. Approximately thirty or so miles from this camp and held in a small compound, were General Wainwright, the Governor of Hong Kong, and several other prominent dignitaries.

At the entrance way, the hospital had an area which we used for sick call. To the rear was a storage room. Along the corridor on the first floor was a room that was supposed to be an operating room with a small room alongside of it that was like a surgical supply room (but without supplies, I might add).

I did a number of operations in the Imperial Army Hospital. The only reason I recall the first one in such detail was because of the experience of having to observe the way Japanese doctors did things. Beside the first case, I recall an appendectomy, gall bladder removal, pleural drainage for infected pleural space, and others. I wondered what was going to happen now that we had this new camp and after I cleared patients who had recovered in the Army Hospital. Luckily, I did not lose one case. I must have had the help of the Big Man upstairs.

On one of the days I came to the hospital, the Japanese dentist acted strange. I kept asking him if I'd done something he didn't approve of, and he kept answering "no." Finally, he told me what was bothering him. He showed me his penis, which had a huge sore, the largest I'd ever seen. I immediately diagnosed it as a syphilitic chancre. He then admitted to me that he'd had sex with a Manchurian girl. I said he should turn in to his sick call officer, but he told me he couldn't do that. The Japanese regulation was that if a soldier contracted a venereal disease from a Japanese woman, he would be treated, but if the disease had been contracted from either a Korean, Manchurian or Chinese woman, the soldier would be thrown in jail and given no treatment whatsoever. For that reason he could not turn himself in.

I asked him if he had any friend in their pharmacy who could be trusted. When he answered yes, I told him to find out if they had Neoarsphenamine (.06 Gm) and if so, to get a syringe and a hypodermic needle. The next day after I finished my rounds, I finally was able to get to his office. He told me he had the medicine and syringe, but was not able to get the .06 grams as the pharmacy only had .03 grams. I told him that it was OK. I would simply double up on injecting it. I gave him two injections per week after he reassured me that his friend would be able to supply him with any amount he needed. With time the big syphilitic sore started melting away, and finally it was gone. He was so grateful and said he didn't know what he could do to return the favor. He again sent everyone from the office, motioned to me to come into the laboratory, and closed the door. He brought out two saki cups and poured some orange juice into them. Then he added a little 95 percent alcohol. He wanted me to celebrate one drink with him. While we were sipping it, he kept telling me not to get drunk because he could get in severe trouble. Some time later, the guard appeared, and off I went, leaving a very happy man.

The next day, after the usual rounds, he said he had permission to take me out of the hospital, but we had to return by a certain time. He drove his car to a two story building near the railroad station and motioned me to come with him. After we went up one flight, he proceeded to rap on a door. When a Japanese girl opened the door and we went in, he said it must have been a long time since I'd had sex and this lady would satisfy me and was clean. I told him I had just gotten married before coming to the Far East and I didn't want to have sex with anyone else. I suggested that he apologize to the woman and we left.

After getting in the car he drove through some narrow streets, and finally stopping at a small one story building. What happened next surprised me. He opened the door with a key and introduced me to another Japanese woman. "I want you to meet my wife," he said. "I have told her all about you." She spoke to me in Japanese as he translated. I realized she was thanking me for all I had done for her husband and I never knew how much he'd told her about the chancre. After a cup of tea he took me back to the hospital.

After our move to the new camp, I continued to go to the Imperial Hospital at intervals doing minor work in our POW camp hospital. Towards evening when we had our sick call, we were always very busy. We were getting to see more of the effects of the extreme cold, specially frost bite. The POWs had to line up in formation early in the morning to stand for "Tenko" (roll call). The Japanese were never in a hurry to come out in the cold and carry out the roll call but they were insistent that the men were out very early. This was just another way they showed the contempt they had for POWs. It was not only that they stood in the cold, they had to march about a mile to the factory. The factory was the MKK. At first the enemy said parts for index machines were made there, but later we found out they were actually airplane parts. The same conditions existed when the men came back from the factory. Most of the men had beards since we had nothing with which to shave. It worried me to see them standing there with their beards a mass of ice. To me it was a miracle that the men could withstand such punishment. If a POW complained that he was ill, the Japanese doctor who was with the inspection team would decide whether or not he could remain behind by just looking at the man with no exam whatsoever.

Chapter 14

An Unusual and Rare Surgical Case

"Whether it be to failure or success, the first need
of being is endurance—we endure with gladness
if we can, with fortitude in any event."

Bliss Carman

I *don't recall just how many* surgical cases I handled, but one stands out in my mind to this day because it was so unusual. One day I was called to the British Officers' quarters to see a colonel who was having unbearable abdominal pains. After checking him over, I decided he had a bowel obstruction. Surgery was clearly indicated. I explained my lack of appropriate medication and that danger existed if I had to resect any bowel. His pain was so severe that he told me to go ahead and do whatever I thought was necessary. He was willing to take the chance rather than continue suffering severe pain and probably die anyway. I had him taken to the camp hospital. I would have preferred to have taken him to the Imperial Army Hospital, but there was no chance of doing that because of the time of day.

We prepared him the best we could and then the question of anesthetic arose. We had some ethyl chloride, a topical anesthetic, which is hardly ever used as a general anesthetic. Dr. Herbst, bless his soul, said he would use it to give drop anesthesia. This would have been a task that even a specialist would have stayed away from because the margin between anesthesia and death was very narrow. He proceeded and finally told me to start. When I opened the abdomen and explored it I felt a mass about the size of a large baseball. That the bowel was distended proximally assured me I'd been right, but what was it? My first thought was that he had some type of tumor. Under the circumstances, I decided to open the bowel and find out what we were dealing with. When I did I found something I had never seen in my entire career. In fact, I had never even heard of such a condition in any surgical manual. When I opened the bowel, I knew I was skating on thin ice because I could easily contaminate the area and cause peritonitis. If that would happen, we had no medication to help. Anyway, what was it? There in my hands lying within the lumen of the bowel was a ball of long worms, exactly like big angle worms. They were knotted together just like angle worms when you use them for fishing. This clump of worms had caused the obstruction. The worms were called ascaris lumbricoides and are very common in the Far East. I removed them all and proceeded to close the bowel and abdominal wall.

During all this time Dr. Herbst was using the ethyl chloride. He gave it so expertly that the patient never turned a hair throughout the procedure. I thought this was a remarkable feat and have talked about it for many years. The patient was returned to a ward, made an uneventful recovery and was back in his barracks in two weeks.

Dear Doctor Shabart

Before we are dispersed & go on separate ways I want to take the opportunity of thanking you again for your kindness and skill in operating on me just a month ago – in the anything but ideal surroundings here. Apart from more serious considerations, it is entirely due to you that I am now on my legs and able to make my inside behave properly at this critical time – and I really am most grateful

I hope we shall meet again.

Yours sincerely,

R G Grimwood

(COLONEL R.R. GRIMWOOD,)
BRITISH ARMY.

To: 1/Lieut. E. J. SHABART,
United States Army Medical Corps.

Letter of gratitude from Colonel Grimwood

Chapter 15

The Imperial Hospital and Trips

"[Courage], a perfect sensibility of the measure of
danger, and a mental willingness to endure it."
William T. Sherman

or some strange reason, I was always treated well
in the Army hospital. Nevertheless, if I asked for
medicine and they had it, they would only give
me one-half the dose we usually used. A little was better
than none, but I couldn't double up on the dose because
when they issued me the drug, it was to last "x" number
of days.

I still couldn't understand why I was never searched
either going to the hospital or coming back. Anyone else
who left the camp was searched thoroughly but they
never as much as touched me. I don't know why.

At one time the truck detoured from its usual route to
the hospital. As I was sitting in the open truck, I noticed
a walled in building when we drove by. As I looked into
the yard, inside the walls I saw what to me must be
Caucasians. Because we were moving so fast, I wasn't
positive. In the short glimpse I saw men, women and
children, which convinced me that maybe this was a civilian internee camp. As a result, I tried to get some bearing

as to where it was in case the need would ever arise later.

When we were in the first camp, the Japanese dentist began to trust me implicitly. One day when I came, he showed me a belt he'd rigged up to which he'd attached a pack of cigarettes, and at times cans of sardines, mandarin oranges or other food. He always had about five cups fastened to the belt. He instructed me to wear it inside my pants, rigging it up in such a way that it didn't bulge. He warned me to be very careful when I got back to camp so I wouldn't be caught with them and to dispose of waste so that it wouldn't be found after I had used the cans. He said if what he gave me was ever discovered, he would be shot. I felt I could be jeopardizing him since when I got through several times with the loot, some of the men would yell out when I came back into the barracks. "Here comes Doc—take down your pants. Let's see what you got." This was always good for a laugh.

I tried to share my good fortune, but how can you be fair when you are living with eighteen others? Major Hankins was the senior officer at the first camp, and for a while in the new camp, until some senior officers came in. The first to outrank him was a British officer. He was not too happy with the amount of rations and felt compelled to complain to the Commandant. Up to this time we officers were not required to work, unless we volunteered. We were given two corn meal buns per day along with our other ration. Workers also received two. The British officer saw the Commandant. When the meeting was over, the officers were granted only one bun per day which didn't sit too well with the others. Yet, this officer had only the interest of the men at heart when he attempted to better conditions.

Considering all the patients I had in the Imperial

Hospital I am happy and grateful that I can say my mortality rate was just about zero. The Big Man upstairs must have been looking over my shoulder. In the Japanese hospital I had less trouble getting what I wanted than I did in the camp. In the camp one terrible Japanese doctor controlled every move. Somehow I found out that his wife was the daughter of a Japanese Admiral. This must have accounted for his Bushido (Emperor deity respect). He gave some medicine at sick call when the spirit moved him. But that was not often. Many POWs suffered untold agony at times due to his lack of caring for the patients' welfare.

Chapter 16

The Camp Hospital

"The Ancient Mariner said to Neptune during a great storm, 'Oh God, you will save me if you wish, but I am going to go on holding my tiller straight.'"

Montaigne

reviously I had described the first floor. The second floor had the wooden beds with the straw mattress on top. Heating was very poor, but at times we could talk the Japanese corps men out of extra blankets. One ward was set aside for our tuberculosis patients. I can't recall one single enemy soldier ever entering that ward—they were deathly afraid of the disease. Every pill given to us was regarded as priceless. We had no intravenous fluids, no blood for transfusions, no antibiotics or other necessities to run a hospital.

A miracle was happening, but at the time we were too busy to think about it. Why didn't we lose more patients when we were treating them without supplies? I felt that God realized we were trying our very best so He too, helped in His own way. Perhaps, after what all these men had gone through, maybe their will to live was greater than anyone could imagine. By the same token, when I was operating, I never thought back to those early days when I'd started in surgery. We had no fancy drugs as they have nowadays. We were taught to treat tissue gently—the less trauma, the less the complications. So really when I think about it now, despite the lack of equipment, it was not so strange my patients usually recovered. I guess I tried to treat the tissue gently, just as I had years before.

If you look at the cover page caricature, you'll notice that I have a pipe in my mouth. Where did a pipe or, for that matter, tobacco come from in a POW camp? An interpreter and a couple of guards would mention to certain of us they were going on a day leave in a couple of days. That was the signal for us to offer some yen to them to bring back a pipe and/or tobacco. I am sure they used the extra money to enhance their leave. They would return, however, with maybe a pipe and Chinese tobacco, which they sneaked into camp. The tobacco was coal black and so strong it would burn your tongue when smoked. It came in a purple bag and because of this and its strong smoke, it acquired the name of "Purple Death." As a rule they did not bring in too many pipes. Some men who wanted to smoke carved their own pipes out of available wood. The Japanese paid us the same basic pay that their officers of the same grade were paid. When we got yen, what else could we do with it but use it to bribe these men to bring back some tobacco. Strange as it may seem, no Japanese officer or guard ever questioned any of us as to where the pipes or tobacco came from. Of course, we did not keep the tobacco packs where they could be easily seen.

At this time, an interesting series of events occurred. Colonel Matsuda, the Commandant, tried to encourage the men to learn Japanese. Since I appeared interested, I was given an index-like large box filled with cards. An

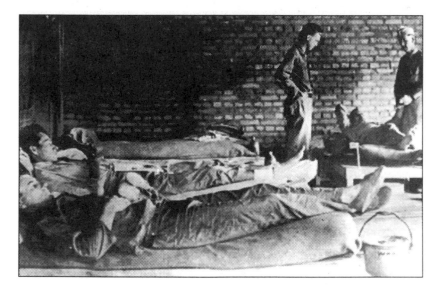

The author (left, standing) and General Gillespie in TB Ward

Italian some years before, whose name was Vicarri, had invented this system to learn Japanese by using the number of strokes in the character. Strokes numbered from one to thirty-two, and each had variations, depending on what characters or strokes were combined with it. This type of language was called Kanji, taken from Chinese characters years and years ago. Later in the centuries, the Japanese added a type of character of their own which is called Katagana. When you read Japanese, you read a combination of both. Interesting, but quite complicated to learn. When I wasn't involved with treating patients, I would go to the second floor office and study the characters, but, of course, no Katanaga. I got quite efficient in interpreting the characters. I was told that the characters were so put together that they produced a picture to the trained eye. For example, the character (人) denotes a tree or wood. However, if you change it to (大), it would mean a stick or to be struck by a stick. I found this all very intriguing.

After a while, Major Hankins and I talked to a POW who worked in a factory office area. The Japanese soldier who worked there would read the "Nippon Times." This paper was like our tabloids in size and came out once a week. There was one section in it that dealt with the enemy war effort. Our POW man offered to hollow out the heel of his shoe and reattach it with screws. Inside the hollow part he would fold a portion of the war effort page which the Japanese would discard. In this way he could pass inspection upon return to camp. He would then give the paper to either the Major or myself. I would eventually try to translate it. There were only eight of us who were aware of what we were doing. Each swore that he would keep all this strictly confidential. We were getting some information at times that was very interesting and encouraging to us. We noted how cleverly they would write about the war progress. Even though at times they would admit to a defeat, they would refer to it as a strategic withdrawal. The paper indicated that the people of Japan should keep the faith and work hard as all was going well as far as the military was concerned. Finally, at one time I got the best news that I had yet been able to translate. The newspaper mentioned that the Japanese Navy had suffered some losses at sea in an area about Formosa. They were going to withdraw from Formosa so as to strengthen their forces elsewhere. They did not mention where. This was the first news we had that the American forces were getting closer and closer to the north. We kept on for a while with translations but finally had to give up when the Japanese soldier apparently was no longer getting the Times.

On occasion, some news drifted out. When the enemy got wind of it, they tried to find out where the information came from. It was always blamed on the Chinese workers in the factory. You might wonder how did they ever know what was going on in our camp. It is with a deep sense of regret and sadness that I must say we did have a very few POW's who were collaborating with the Japanese in return for special favors. Eventually, we found out who they were and when the war was over, they were brought to trial in the States.

Chapter 17

The Camp Bomb

"History is a vast early warning system."
Norman Cousins

t was sometime towards the end of 1944 around the 7th of December, that a warning was sounded in the camp. The men ran out of the barracks. There in the sky we saw bombers approaching in our direction. The men spread out on the parade ground while all the Japanese disappeared. A factory located about one-half mile from us which we had believed was an ammunition plant was hit. This factory was one in which our men did not work. It was only partly visible from the upper floors of the barracks. One of the bombers was lagging behind and was dipping its wings. At first, we cheered because we thought he was trying to tell us that they knew about us. Our camp had no POW markings. However, all of a sudden, a five hundred pound bomb came from the plane, landing in the middle of our parade grounds.

At the siren the corps men and doctors all went to the hospital for cover, but after the bomb was dropped, we realized we had a massive task on our hands.

One of our men who had been in the air force told me that the reason the pilot was tipping his wings back and forth was to try and release a bomb that was stuck. As it would happen, when it did shake loose, it came down diagonally and landed amongst the men. It was not a sight one could easily forget. As I remember, fourteen men were killed outright. Approximately sixty were injured, to a greater or less degree, with twenty-three needing surgery without any question. All the wounded were brought into the hospital and were spread out on the floor where sick call had always been held. There would be one body lying alongside another, so close that you had trouble stepping over them to evaluate the condition of any patient. In this triage area I must commend the many volunteers who brought the wounded in and who did the best they could to follow our orders to give first aid while we tried to sort out priority cases for surgery. We had our work cut out for us, but what about the supplies we would need? No blood, nothing to treat shock. Bleeding had to be controlled for the most part by compression of the areas. Worst of all, we realized we had no anesthetic, nothing but ethyl chloride, which is used as a topical anesthetic, not as a general. Dr. Herbst again rose to the occasion and said he would use it and drip drop it over a bandage in the manner in which ether was used years ago. As I have said, anyone who knows anything about ethyl chloride knows that if used in that manner, the borderline between anesthesia and death from heart arrest is very, very narrow. I doubt if we would have had a specialist in that field who would have wanted to use it. Dr. Herbst went ahead. During this time, we were preparing the operative site.

I shall never forget the first case we selected and over

the subsequent years there was more to tell about him. His name was Baumgartner, and his nickname in the camp was "Bum." While the corpsmen were sterilizing our inadequate instruments, I evaluated the nature of his severe arm wound. The upper part of his arm was badly mangled. The fragment of bomb that hit him had torn the bone to shreds, as well as the soft tissue. His arm was just limp, with no circulation whatsoever. Amputation was indicated. One was tempted to do so at the shoulder, but the more I thought about it, I decided to try and leave a short stump so that if all went well, maybe some day he could use a prosthesis. I could not create flaps, nor did I want to because of the fear of severe infection and especially gas gangrene. I did what is known as a guillotine type. In this procedure one cuts straight across the limb, shortens the bone slightly, controls bleeding and places ties around the nerves to decrease post operative nerve pain. Of course, the healing process is very slow, because the skin has to cross the raw area and heal from side to side, sometimes never doing it completely. I finished the procedure without any adverse problem. When we selected "Bum," we noted an injury to his temple area which, however, did not appear to be too important, what with a man having a useless arm dangling, as his did.

However, when I finished, Dr. Herbst said to me, "Shay, take a look at this." I looked over at his head, and there was this head wound, measuring about one and a half inch by one inch. Through it was bulging a small portion of his brain. The bomb fragment had also torn a small piece of his skull away, but with all this there was very little bleeding. The brain had not been bulging out at the start. I looked at Herbst and remember saying, "This is one hell of a deal." Since we had no special instruments, I did the only thing I could do—a clean debridement of the wound. This meant I would clear away any badly damaged tissue so as to leave neat, clean wound edges. I would remove only the non-viable tissue. I'd then put a sterile dressing on it and begin to wonder if this would be enough to save the man. But there wasn't much time to think. I had to remember there were more men awaiting surgery in the triage area.

Over the many weeks I watched "Bum," he got better and better, so much so that I found it hard to believe, considering that the surgery had been so primitive.

Dr. Herbst, myself, and several corpsmen worked for three days and nights trying to save whatever we could of the remaining twenty-two men. Sadly, some amputations were necessary. We had no sleep and very little to eat. In between cases, we would sit in the small room next to the OR and wait for the few instruments we had to get sterilized by boiling them in water over a charcoal burner. After a while, all of us began to notice we were getting dizzy and feeling like we were going to pass out. What was going on? Was it lack of sleep, lack of food, or what? I agonized about working with such limited supplies. All of a sudden, it dawned on us that the open charcoal burner in this small room was throwing off carbon monoxide. Since there was no ventilation we were getting carbon monoxide poisoning. In spite of the cold outside, we had to change our procedure slightly opening the window at intervals to get fresh, cold air and keeping the door open.

Every type of wound injury was handled with Dr. Herbst giving the anesthesia. He had a tough job and mine was not any easier. We had no trained assistant or instrument nurse, yet, in spite of what seemed like impossible conditions, men were getting better. There are no words that I can use to commend the corpsmen enough for the dedication they showed. Dr. Herbst, who administered the problematic ethyl chloride, was fabulous. Frankly, I don't know how he did it.

Again, with the help of the Big Man upstairs, I am happy to say I had twenty-two of the twenty-three cases survive. The one case I lost was an Australian, a very likable chap. The poor fellow developed gas gangrene in his leg. I did what is known as a fasciotomy, which means opening up the various planes between the muscle layers with large incisions through the skin and down into the planes. The idea is to allow the gas, as it develops, to escape. I had my doubts that I would be able to save him. For one thing, I had no gas gangrene antitoxin. Within three days we lost him, the only one of the bombing surgical cases that didn't make it.

Considering all these surgeries were conducted under anything but desirable conditions, we must have had God on our side. We had no sterile gowns, no sterile rubber gloves, no way to give adequate preoperative preparation, and no available blood for transfusions or any intravenous solutions. Nor did we have anti-infection drugs. The Japanese relied on a type of sulfa drug, but none was given to me for my patients. Believe me, I had none available. During all these events, it was very interesting that the Japanese, who disappeared so suddenly when the bomb dropped, were nowhere to be seen for almost three days. We wondered where they were hiding.

Literally all the POW's pitched in to help get the wounded to our little hospital, doing whatever we told them to control bleeding and other life threatening problems. Boxie Bocksell was one of the tireless workers who stayed through the entire ordeal in the triage area. I always felt the other POWs deserved a great share of credit for our low mortality rate. I could never understand why we didn't lose men in shock. Maybe what the POWs had gone through before gave them such a desire to live that it made them strong.

Chapter 18

Mukden

"Courage is doing what you're scared to do. There can be no courage unless you're scared."
Eddie Rickenbacker

Mukden was a large city spread out like Chicago. In the center was the old walled city. The walled city in early days and before the Japanese occupation was called Hoten. There were four entrances to it—the East, West, North and South gates. I was told that the Japanese were under orders never to go into it alone or with less than a squad of men. They learned the hard way—when their men tried to go in alone or with a small group, they never came out again. Mukden contained the royal Manchurian castle, a beautiful place, with courtyards surrounding it and all the amazing exterior painting of mostly greens, reds, and yellows. The carvings took our breath away. This castle housed the last of the Manchu Dynasty. The Japanese had sealed the building. Anyone entering would be shot. However, the real valuables in the Temple had been removed by the Manchurians and hidden before the Japanese invaded the country. Mukden was second in size only to Harbin.

Chapter 19

The Missing Planing Machine

"There are some people that if they don't know,
you can't tell 'em."

Louis Armstrong

O *ne day at the factory* a detail of men was selected
to dig a certain size hole in the ground and work
along with some Chinese workers. After the
hole was dug, it was to be filled with concrete to form the
foundation for a large planing machine. One of the
Americans always ran the overhead crane in this part of
the factory.

One of the customs the Japanese had was to appear at
a Bushido meeting every noon after lunch. This was a
pep rally and always lasted the same length of time. They
were constantly encouraged in these meetings, to speed
up production to better help their Empire. A bell would
ring, calling them to the meeting, and would ring again
when they should return to work.

Our men conceived a brilliant plan. When the hole
was dug to the required specifications, the men would
have concrete ready to pour. The man operating the crane
was given the signal and raised up this heavy plane
machine and dropped it into the hole at the same time

the men were pouring the concrete over it to fill the hole. They completed this work just as the bell rang, for the Japanese foreman to return. As he did, they were busy leveling the concrete. When he saw that the foundation was already in, he was overcome with joy to think that the POWs had done their job so quickly. The concrete was to set for several days, and then the foreman was going to place the plane machine on it. Several days later, when the men came to work, there was turmoil. The Japanese didn't know where they had last put the machine. In trying to ask the men they got only "I don't know" for an answer.

They never did find out. I think to this day, if the factory is still standing, the plane machine must still be buried in its concrete bed. This hearty, yet dangerous prank showed our men had retained both their sense of humor and their bravery. It was kept secret for as long as necessary. I guess the statute of limitations has long since passed.

Chapter 20
New Neighbors

"The enemy of my enemy is my friend."

Arabic proverb

Sometime in late 1944, about fifteen Americans arrived. They were not put in our camp, but in a small compound across the street. Our windows, which faced in that direction, were boarded up because of our captor's effort to prevent any communication with them. Our cook house was ordered to send one bucket of food daily to them, along with anything else the Japanese would approve. The bucket would be returned to our camp at the end of the day. Again, the POWs arose to the occasion by creating a secret space at the bottom of the bucket in which a note could be slipped. The men across the way caught on and so a line of communication developed. They were air force men who'd been shot down and were kept in secret at this place. They had been horribly treated when they were first taken prisoner and were in poor physical shape.

Chapter 21
Other New Arrivals

"A high station in life is earned by the gallantry with which appalling experiences are survived with grace."

Tennessee Williams

t seemed like everything was happening in 1944. A group of senior officers arrived who had been kept at Formosa until their hurried evacuation. They were the American General Clifford Bluemel, General Keith Simmons of the Royal British Service, General De Fremery of the Royal Dutch Expeditionary Forces, Colonel John Pugh, the Aide de Camp to General Wainwright, and many more from these different countries. They were kept in a separate section of the barracks.

This same year we were instructed to have everything in top-top shape as the International Red Cross was coming through to inspect conditions in the camp. We hoped this would be the break we'd been waiting for. The day arrived. There were four men representing the International Red Cross from Switzerland. The Camp Commandant and his staff joined them as they toured the camp. When they came to the hospital, they stopped and talked to me and asked if there was anything I needed. I began to hope. The leader said, "Make out a list and bring it to Japanese headquarters" later that day. I did so, and rushed over with the list. Nothing ever arrived. I didn't know if supplies were sent and the enemy kept them. The following year, when I was asked the same question by another group from Switzerland, I told them I was still waiting for last year's list to be delivered. They didn't act surprised or show any emotion, but I don't think the Camp Commandant liked what I said as told to him by the interpreter.

Chapter 22

Medicine and Packages from Home

"Dignity does not consist in possessing honors, but in deserving them."

Aristotle

e were told that packages had arrived from the United States and would be distributed before too long. Days seemed like years before they were distributed. Again, the Japanese did not show concern for us. They would take twenty to thirty packages at random and empty their contents on a long table. Each package was in a pile. The camp number of the POW was placed on the pile. The lucky men would be called. This continued for many days. The Japanese removed cigarettes and chocolate or any other candy. Of course, we had no idea what was sent to us in the first place, but those items were always missing.

I remember my package. In it my wife had sent me a pair of olive military slacks. I sure appreciated them. Another thing she sent was the upper portion of thermal underwear. This was really great in the cold of this country. However, I was mad that there were no bottoms, and accused our captors of pilfering them. I might as well tell you now that in the bottom of the olive pants leg she had stashed powdered quinine. Unfortunately, I never discovered it. I had the pants shortened and hence the quinine was never found even by our camp tailor. Much later, she told me she never sent the thermal bottoms because they were limited by box size as to what they could send.

Apparently what also came on the Red Cross ship "Gripsholm" with these packages was a variety of medications. They were put in the warehouse to the rear of the first floor in the hospital. After a wait of some days, our captors asked for the doctors to come with them to this room. Three of us went under heavy guard and were told to open up the various bottles and count whatever there was in them. If the bottle said 100 tablets, and we counted only 98, they became angry and accused us of stealing the missing ones. If the bottle contained 102, that was OK with them. We tried to explain to the guards that in America these bottles are filled by machine. It was therefore normal to have a few more or less than the actual label showed. Much to our sorrow, we were told we could request the medicine for a given patient, but the camp Japanese doctor would have to approve before it would be released. We were frustrated again and again by this terrible doctor who hated every last one of us.

One day we were summoned to the so-called recreation room where the Japanese had on display a variety of paintings on silk in the form of scrolls. They told us they had been in an art display and were signed. We could purchase one per POW officer if we desired. They were all different. I selected one that was painted by a Tamikawa Koyo and was supposedly displayed at Daidoten Donin. It was entitled "Leaping Carp." We paid for the scrolls with the yen we were accumulating. This act of the Japanese remains a mystery to me to this day. Why this sudden display of kindness? They claimed they wanted us to learn to appreciate Japanese art. I wonder about it and never had an answer. I have never framed mine. It does display the original form translated as above and contains a seal of being authentic as well as my POW number "Four."

Chapter 23

Dentistry at Its Best

"Deep experience is never peaceful"

Henry James

One day, when sick call was about over, General Bluemel came to me with something clutched in his hand. He offered it and showed me a gold inlay that had fallen out. He pleaded with me to please try and reinsert it so he would not lose the tooth. I told him to return the next night and bring the inlay with him. I remembered that in the warehouse I had seen zinc oxide and Nujol oil. I also recalled that when I was a kid and went to the dentist, if he was going to put a temporary filling in your tooth, he would take a small amount of zinc oxide and place it on a small glass plate. He would then add a few drops of Nujol and mix them together to make the paste to put into the cavity. It would harden after a while and usually stayed until you were due to return. Somehow I convinced a Japanese corpsman to give me just a very little of the zinc oxide and a little of the oil. Then, before the General came that night, I also obtained a little alcohol and a bit of carbolic acid.

When the General showed up as agreed, I took him

into a side room and proceeded to do my first bit of dentistry. I touched the inside of the cavity with the carbolic acid and immediately neutralized it with alcohol. then I made a paste as described before and filled the cavity with the paste. Finally I took the inlay, pressed it into the cavity with the paste, and held it there for a brief period of time. I folded a small gauze bandage into a roll, placed it into his mouth over the inlay area and had him bite down on it. I told him to keep biting on it for about two hours until the paste would set.

For about a year or more, until the time we were liberated, the inlay stayed in place. The General was so pleased after a month or two that he insisted that I disregard the General business and call him by his nickname, "Blinky." I replied that I respected his rank so it would be hard to call him by that name. He said, "Yes, but your friendship means more to me than you calling me General." From that time on he was "Blinky," except when we were in the presence of other ranking senior officers.

While we are on the subject of dentistry, I should mention that we had no dental officer in our camp, yet, we had many men turn up with severe toothaches. When this occurred in a badly decayed tooth, it meant only one thing—an extraction. We had a special chair made of wood which was used mostly for extractions. It was built in a semi-reclining position. The unlucky man was told to lie down on it. Usually two corps men would hold his body and head while we proceeded to extract the tooth. We used no anesthetic because we had none to use. As the saying goes, you grin and bear it just to get rid of the toothache. As close as I can remember, Dr. Herbst pulled about three hundred teeth in that manner while I think I pulled about half that number.

For extractions there are usually left and right extractors, depending on which side one would do the extraction. We only had a left. We used it to extract teeth, whether it was on the left or right side. It made no difference as we developed our own art in pulling teeth. I think we got so adept at it that we could have used an ordinary pliers if we had to.

All of these extractions happened without incident except on one occasion. Dr. Herbst told me that the root and base of a rotten tooth had broken off and broke into the maxillary sinus, which lies below the cheek bones. We felt if we left it there, serious infection could occur. I recalled an operation called a Caldwell-Luc in which the base of the sinus was entered into through an incision made between the gum and cheek. Again, our two man team went to work and the root was removed. All went well and no complications developed.

Chapter 24

The Impossible Made Possible

"The paradox of courage is that a man must be a little careless of his life even in order to keep it."

G.K. Chesterton

bout this time, one of the POW's was brought to our hospital in bad shape. Apparently he'd been working on a spinning machine at a textile factory, and somehow his hand got caught in the machine. He had a dirty, bloody old rag held over his hand. He was as pale as a ghost. When I looked at it, I told Dr. Herbst that the soldier had done such a job on his hand it looked like nothing short of an amputation could be done. He was taken to our small operating room and prepared in our usual manner. As I evaluated the hand once more, I decided to do something which I think even to this day I might hesitate to do. I decided to try and save his thumb and little finger. They both seemed to have good color and circulation and he did appear to have feeling in them. I decided to amputate the second, third, and fourth fingers at least a good halfway up his hand. If I had enough viable skin for partial closure and if I was lucky, he would probably wind up using the two fingers like pinchers. I thought this would be a good deal better than amputating the entire hand and eventually he might be blessed with trying to use an artificial hand.

I proceeded with the operation, which was very difficult because of continuing lack of instruments. We finished the job and all went quite well. He was sent upstairs to begin what I had hoped would be another good recovery. By now you can begin to gather that because I had so little in the way of medical supplies, I was beginning to rely more and more on God's help. The patient was watched very closely. As the days went by, he gradually began healing to a point that I wouldn't have thought possible. No infection or complication set in. In roughly a month he began to develop motion in the two fingers and as time went on, he eventually was able to use them as I had originally hoped.

Chapter 25

Some Thoughts in Retrospect

"Experience, which destroys innocence, also leads
people back to it."

James Baldwin

As I now *think back* on all the traumatic surgery
with considerable bleeding, especially in the
bombing incident, and all the other emergency
surgery, it makes me wonder how so much of this took
place without the usual support. No matter what the procedure, just as stated before, we had no blood for transfusions, no intravenous fluids, no antibiotics, bandages or
rubber gloves. Sterile gowns or drapes were not available.
I have to ask myself, "How in the world did I get by with
so low a mortality rate?" Some supernatural spirit had to
be looking over my shoulder at all times. It seems like this
was the only explanation I can give.

As a doctor I was really grateful to the men in camp
who were so helpful in assisting us after the bombing,
and carrying out our orders tirelessly. Remember, though
none of them had ever had any such experiences in the
past, they had to make bandages, tourniquets or whatever, the best they knew how. What a remarkable job was
done. The mortality of that incident speaks for itself.

The one who was lost and died of gas gangrene in his leg did so simply because we had no antitoxin against gangrene. There was one thing I learned way back. When dealing with a traumatic wound, one does not try to close up the wounds tightly. It is best if necessary to do a careful debridement and leave the wound open. Debridement in such cases meant to cut away all non-viable tissue and leave the wound surfaces with clean, healthy looking tissue. That is why in all of the cases of severe trauma I tried to do exactly that.

As I think back, it seems to me that at the start of the war, when we were in Bataan, the base hospitals were doing their share to get the word out not to sew up wounds—just leave them open—if possible, primarily to avoid gangrene.

Chapter 26

Parachute Visitors and Russians

"Democracy is a small hard core of common agreement, surrounded by a rich variety of individual differences."

James Bryant Conant

*O*ne day it became kind of obvious that the war might be coming to an end. You can imagine how we felt. On this particular day, about six Americans parachuted into the Mukden area. They were taken prisoner and brought to our camp, along with some of their equipment. We suspected that maybe even our captors were getting the word that things were not going well for the Empire. Oddly, these men were given a great deal of freedom in camp, but were cautiously communicative to us. As I remember, they even had a small radio allowed into the camp for their use. They were given special quarters in the hospital so as to make communication with us more difficult.

The Russians declared war on Japan August 8, 1945. It is interesting to point out that the Russians entered the war two days after we dropped the atom bomb on Hiroshima. On August 16th we found out that the war was over, the official surrender being August 14th. We are told that the Emperor desired to surrender, but his advisory committee was split 3-3 to reject the Potsdam Alternatives. With the 3-3 split the committee wished to continue the fight. On August 9th, the second atomic bomb was dropped on Nagasaki. It was then that the Emperor of Japan, by decree, declared the surrender. Of course, this displeased the committee.

We knew for sure it was all over when American planes flew over and parachuted food and medical supplies to us. About the same time, a Russian tank battalion came to the camp and took the Japanese prisoners. The Russian soldiers rounded them up on the parade grounds and giving us their Japanese guns told us to go ahead and shoot them. We declined, telling them we did not live by that creed. After our answer they marched them away, and we never saw them again. I have seen tough looking men in my day, but the toughest looking men I had ever seen were in this tank outfit.

Somewhere along the line we found out that when the Russians declared war, they'd attacked the Japanese along the Siberian-Manchurian border. They had been instructed at the earliest possible time, by General MacArthur, to proceed to the compound holding General Wainwright and other high ranking officers, and then to our camp after freeing them. It was common knowledge that orders had been given to liquidate all POW's in the event of a surrender. General MacArthur was understandably concerned that they might not hesitate in the camps to carry out the order to liquidate us in any way the Camp Commandant felt feasible.

On my first return trip to Mukden after the surrender, I remember passing many truckloads of soldiers—all in new looking uniforms—all Asians—all wearing a baseball-like cap with a red star on the front. They all appeared well armed. There were twenty to thirty men to each truck and each was speeding to a different location.

One of the men who came into Mukden Camp was an American dentist. There wasn't much he could do in the way of help since no dental instruments were available. However, he came with a bunch of Chiang Kai Shek gold paper currency. Although this looked very impressive, it was military money with little backing. Interestingly, the Manchurians did not know that.

One day he asked if he and I could get into the walled city. I said, "No problem." He felt maybe we could pick up some valuable Chinese articles using the impressive gold paper currency. We went into the walled city and wandered around. Soon a Manchurian led us through a few courtyards into a Chinese house. The person who lived there took up the floor boards and showed us some articles from the Manchu castle. The dentist bought an egg shell porcelain tea set and I bought a heart shaped opal ring to bring home to my wife. I'd begun to hope I'd actually see her again. We were told it had been worn by the Manchu Princess. He also told us the Temple was mostly cleaned out of valuables before the Japanese got into Mukden.

We left feeling good, but as we were preparing to exit from the walled city, two tough looking characters motioned us to follow them. Frightened, we did, wondering what we'd got into. We finally were taken into a house, where about twenty Manchurians were lying around in a room filled with smoke. In the next room there was a Russian who had us sit across a table from him. "What are you up to, where did you come from?" were some of the questions he asked. He had piercing eyes that made you feel he was looking straight through your head.

When we finally convinced him we had no secret mission, he had a bottle of vodka brought out. He insisted we each have a drink with him, giving a "Salute to Stalin and Roosevelt." He then offered to have us driven to our camp but we declined, saying we needed exercise.

Many months later, as I reflected on the truckloads of soldiers and the incident with the tough interrogator, I realized that the Russians had infiltrated Manchuria during the Japanese occupation. Then they'd set up cadres of soldiers to take over in the event the Japanese Empire should fall. This, of course, was all secret. These cadres were centered in the walled city where the Japanese did not wish to enter. I found out that the racing trucks were intended to take over government buildings, police stations, railroad lines, and radio stations, as well as to clean up on any resisting Japanese. Talk about your James Bond intrigue! This was a well planned organization that knew every move the Japanese made. Their spies were all Manchurians, not Russians, and could get about Manchuria without being detected as spies.

Chapter 27

The Last Trip to the Army Imperial Hospital

"Truth is the only merit that gives dignity and worth to history."

Lord Acton

he day after we heard of the surrender, I returned to the Army Hospital taking a tough looking American First Sergeant with me. I didn't want to go alone and thought I might need a little protection. Two naturally being better than one in terms of defense, we went first to the dentist's office but as soon as we arrived, the dentist told me that the Commanding Officer wanted to see me in his office immediately.

He took both of us through the corridors of the hospital and stopped at one door on the top floor where he rapped and we went in. It was a large room with no furnishings whatsoever, just a desk on the far side near the windows and a chair in which the Colonel was sitting. To our left, as we entered, were two files of fifteen officers, each standing at attention. This was totally unexpected. I was terrified. What in the world had I gotten myself and the sergeant into?

The Colonel stood up and made a speech in Japanese, which was interpreted by the dentist. The gist of it was that they had received word the Russians had entered Mukden and would be showing up at the hospital in a few hours. He said as officers they valued their Samurai swords more than life itself. The swords had a history all their own. Some of them dating back to the days of the Samurai era. On each metal handle was an inscription telling of the warrior who had used it and when. On each side of the handle was some kind of metal that surrounded the sword handle. It was held together on each side by Minuki. If one unscrewed the Minuki, the sides would fall away, leaving the metal handle of the sword with the inscription visible as described. He said since they valued the swords so much, they did not, under any circumstances, want them to fall into the hands of the Russians. He said they knew of my work in the hospital and my integrity as a surgeon. They would consider it an honor if I would accept their swords. They knew that I would respect them and they could rest in their minds that all were in good, trusted hands.

This was the last thing I expected, and it left me speechless. When the dentist told me that the Colonel was awaiting my reply, I gathered my thoughts quickly. I had the interpreter tell him I would be honored to accept their swords. They could also rest assured the swords would always be treated with respect and never degraded. After that translation the Japanese Colonel stepped from behind his desk and walked up to us. He stood erect in front of me as he unlatched his sword. Then, with outstretched hands, he presented the sword to me while he was bowing. Again, I almost fell over as I never had one of our captors bow to me. I returned the bow, after he finished, but it felt really strange. When he went back to his desk, he barked out some kind of order which was not translated to me. The officers, who were lined up, came up, one by one, and offered me their sword in the same manner complete with the bow. It became a bizarre ritual, almost like a dance as I always returned the bow after receiving the sword. The swords eventually became so heavy that I had to turn some of them over to the sergeant to help hold them since I did not want to degrade them by setting any one of them on the floor.

When this ceremony was over, the Colonel again stood up and told us through the interpreter that he wished us well—not only us, but all the POW's in our camp. I then told them that I hoped they would also be well treated in whatever lay ahead of them, especially since they were medical officers and, as such, were non-combatants. With that and a farewell bow, it was over. As I walked away, knowing how much they were hated by the Russians, I wondered what would really happen to them.

This entire procedure was so full of respect, so unlike the previous encounters with Japanese soldiers that I think I left the room actually feeling a degree of sorrow for them. It wasn't until many months later that I found out what had happened.

We went back to camp and hid the swords. I gave one to the Sergeant and had to decide what to finally do with the others.

I thought about these swords a lot and finally decided some of these elderly men, officers who had made the military their career, should be remembered. They had gone through so much to survive. Wouldn't it be nice to give certain of them a samurai sword so they could carry it back as a souvenir of things gone by? I gave the Hospital Commandant's sword to General Bluemel. Then I gave swords to some of the others, ones I knew

had done their best for the men. It was such a good feeling to see their faces light up. They had a rich token. For
some reason it made me happy to give them away.

I figured I would leave one for myself.

Chapter 28

The Feast and Medicine

"War does not determine who is right—only who is left."

Anonymous

ome supplies of food flown in to us had been distributed to the men, but when we saw Spam, we went crazy with delight. Along with all the rest of the canned food, it turned out to be the feast of a lifetime. We ate and ate, trying to make up for literally years of being hungry. Then the men began to pay the penalty, and the doctors got extra busy again. Since we hadn't had meat for so long or such big servings, the digestive system of many men rebelled. We saw acute distentions of the stomach as well as acute indigestion, all from eating too much and too fast.

One thing that happened after the surrender was that finally, all the medicine in the warehouse came under our control. We began to practice medicine with a little more usefulness. Every time I saw a bottle of aspirin, I would suddenly recall getting threatened by our captors because the count at opening the bottle was only nine hundred and ninety eight instead of the thousand that the label indicated.

Within a few days of the surrender our senior officer asked me to go to Mukden to see if I could locate the internee camp and find out what was needed. I told him I thought I knew the approximate location. I was given a truck and took a corpsman with me to help.

Sure enough, the internees were Caucasians—men, women, and children. When we entered the courtyard, we were greeted with cheers, hugs and even kisses. They said they hadn't seen anyone but Japanese soldiers while in their enclosure. Unless there were other camps that we didn't know about, we were the first to find the internees.

They took us into this large building where they all lived together in an auditorium like room. Everyone slept on the floor. Families stayed together and had strung blankets or sheets between them for some degree of privacy. They were a delightful group, so grateful to have been found. In talking to some of them who knew English, I discovered they were missionaries from Belgium, France and Italy.

In checking them medically I could see that overall they were in poor physical condition. It was obvious that they needed some good food and certain medicines. I told them that I'd return very soon with all they needed. It was a very emotional scene. One mother said something to her young daughter, who grabbed my leg when I was leaving and gave it a big hug. I almost broke out in tears.

When I made my return visit, they were waiting anxiously. They even asked me to stay a while and share a meal with the food that was brought for them. Knowing how badly they needed the food, I declined.

Buddhist God of Fertility

Chapter 29
My Tour of Mukden — Surprise!

"Life begins on the other side of despair"
Jean Paul Sartre

fter leaving the internee camp, I went into the main business area of Mukden where the Mukden Hotel was located.

The hotel was similar in structure to our hotels, six or eight stories high. When I wandered through the various floors, I was surprised to find that you couldn't flush the toilet above the third floor. Their water pressure systems didn't have enough power to handle flushing at the higher levels.

While I was walking around in the lobby, I was approached by a Manchurian who was neatly dressed in Western clothes. Since he could speak English, we sat down and had a nice conversation. I found out that before the Japanese occupation of Manchuria he had been the general distributor for Ford products in that area.

He invited me to his home and introduced me to his wife, also a Manchurian, who spoke no English. She served us tea and some form of cracker. After a bit she asked him something, I guess in Manchurian. He told me she wanted to know if my wife and I had any children. I explained that I'd only been married less than three months before being sent to the Far East—the Philippines—and captured. If my wife had given birth to a baby after I left, I didn't know about it. I understood not a word of the next brief discussion between my host and hostess. They then got up and walked over to a Chinese shrine in the corner of the room where we were sitting. They took out a bronze statue—talked some more and then handed it to me. My host said his wife wanted me to have it. It was the Buddhist God of Fertility. He said that I should take it home with me—and the first child we'd have would be a boy, a healthy boy. I will add here that after I finally returned to the States, our first and only child was a boy. Was it just coincidence, or did the God of Fertility play a part? All these years later we still display the bronze on our fireplace mantle.

It was a very cordial and delightful afternoon, but the time finally came when I had to head back to camp before dark. I never saw or heard from them again. I gave my address to them when I left and they gave me theirs. Unfortunately, I lost theirs. I hope they did well. They were a delightful couple and really touched my heart.

Chapter 30

The Evaluation for Evacuation

"It is not the years in your life but the life in your years that counts."

Adlai Stevenson

he time finally came when we were given orders to plan to evacuate the camp. It became necessary to sort out the patients among the POW's on a priority basis. The most seriously ill and most recent surgical cases were to be flown out by our planes. The second group, who were not critically ill, were to be transported out to meet up with a hospital ship. The remainder were to leave via military transports. Naturally some of the men tried to get into the priority category in order to speed going home. Of course, we could show no favoritism.

While doing this work with the other doctors, I was approached one night by one of the ranking Colonels. He told me that twelve Colonels were under orders to remain behind and do some G2 work. (This means intelligence service.) These orders, he said, were received from Headquarters. He then explained that the twelve were going to be there all alone without any medical man to help if they got sick. Did they think in Headquarters that no one would get sick, so there would be no need for a medical doctor? As the Colonel talked I stood listening and wondering why they were telling me all this. Then my unspoken question was answered. I was asked if I could consider staying behind with them since they would feel so much safer knowing they had me with them in case one of them needed medical help.

I thought for a bit and then asked how long their mission was going to take. He assured me that they would be finished in two weeks and then all arrangements for our return would be expedited. I pondered again for a short while and then told them I had a wife waiting for me who was probably just as anxious as their own families. My wife would be wondering, for sure, why I was not returning like the rest. I finally realized they were equally concerned about returning and since things would be expedited after the mission, told them I would stay. That brought me a tremendous handshake from several of them as well as a warm hearted slap on the back. I could see they were relieved and I had a feeling again of doing something good.

Things did not work out as planned, and the mission took about three weeks to complete. I never asked what the mission was, nor did they ever tell me. Later I will tell what finally came to my mind as to their purpose.

Chapter 31

A Gift from Senior Officers

"Too much happens...Man performs, engenders
so much more than he can or should have to bear.
That's how he finds that he can bear anything."
William Faulkner

hen the work was done and we were getting ready to leave, I was approached by the group of twelve. At the request of the Generals and themselves, I was to be given a set of two boxes of surgical instruments that had been found in a separate room at Japanese headquarters. They really were two boxes comprising what was called Japanese Army Field Hospital Instruments. They contained instruments of every kind, capable of doing any and all types of surgery, even including brain and orthopedic work. In all that time of captivity I never knew they had the instruments in the camp. I guess the Japanese were saving it only for their own use. It hurt badly remembering how I did all the surgery with so few improvised instruments.

Each case was very heavy. They measured about two feet by one and a half feet, and were about eighteen inches tall. I noticed that the instruments were placed in the box with absolute precision so if you took any out and did not replace them exactly as they had been before, you would be left with some with no place to put them. It was really a masterpiece of planning to arrange them so meticulously.

After I accepted the gifts I asked how in the world I was going to get them all the way back home. They told me they would help carry them until we got to Okinawa. From there, arrangements would be made to ship them to my home. I said "fine," and began to wonder how we were going to travel.

We left camp by truck and boarded a train at the Mukden Station. I understand the train was supplied by the Russians. There were only two cars and our car had plush seats which reminded me of old fashioned parlor cars with the individual seats that rotated around in any direction. I don't know where the Russians got them. Unfortunately, the engine was sure having trouble. It leaked water badly. At every water stop it was necessary to fill the tanks. The care of such equipment must have been a problem for the Japanese in their occupation. At any rate we finally reached Dairen, Korea where an American Attack Transport was waiting. We were welcomed aboard with great cheers and the two boxes of instruments and my one remaining samurai sword followed us. I hid the samurai sword under the mattress of my bunk while the instrument boxes were taken care of by navy personnel. They then fed us such a feast that to this day I can see that table of food. It was like something we had dreamed of. The officers aboard treated us with dignity. After eating our fill, we came up with a name for the group, which followed us all the way to the Philippines. We called ourselves the "Lucky Thirteen." That name was soon to be tested.

Midway between Dairen and Okinawa, as we were sailing in mine infested fields, a typhoon suddenly blew

Japanese Army Filed Hospital Instruments

in. The deck men tried shooting the mines with guns on deck as they were spotted. What followed were the worst waves I have ever seen, and I thought I had seen them all. The waves were at least five stories high, or maybe even higher. The ship just slid up and down the sides of these huge waves as it slowly plowed ahead. It was no place to be if you suffered from sea sickness.

Someone spotted a floating mine on one of the waves. It was sliding down the wave towards the ship and there was nothing one could have done to avoid it. Three sailors looking over the side of the ship were watching the mine when suddenly, it hit us midship and decapitated the three sailors. It was an agonizing sight. I was then told that everyone in the engine room had been killed. That was the place where the mine had hit. Meantime, other sailors were frantically shoring up the compartment walls between the fore and aft holds and the mid-compartment using long wooden beams. This action kept us afloat even though we had no power. The hole in the midship was estimated to be about eighteen feet wide. It was frightening to see water rush in and out.

A few other sailors and marines were injured, some requiring surgery. I immediately went to the OR area and began to help treat the worst emergency cases. An SOS had been sent out right after the explosion, but it was a while before a cruiser pulled into the area. Even then because of the huge waves and wind, it could not get too close to us, so they tried shooting a cable. No luck—the wind was too strong and simply blew it away from our ship. Any chance of a hookup was impossible. Finally, a large tug appeared. We were told it came from Okinawa. Luckily, it did manage to get close enough to latch on with a cable. As it towed us through the huge waves and heavy wind I was amazed that it could weather these waves and wind. Finally, it towed us into Naha Bay, where we dropped anchor. The wind had let up quite a bit by now and the waves were not quite so high. I noticed all the ships that had been anchored in the Bay had gone out to deeper waters so the wind could not bump them against each other. The thirteen of us left the ship along with my boxes of instruments. As I raised my mattress to take my sword, I was unpleasantly surprised. Wow—the sword was gone. You can be sure I tore that bunk apart. No luck. Anyway I had the instruments.

The way we disembarked was a new experience for me. We had to crawl down the side of the ship on rope ladders. Because of the two heavy boxes and the curve of the ship's side, it was not exactly an easy way to get off. We all thanked the Lord when we were on solid ground once again. Meantime I was told that someone was taking the instrument boxes to Headquarters where they'd be properly packed and shipped to my home. At least that was no problem.

Eventually we boarded a truck that took us into a different camp where we were given clean, dry uniforms. Of course, when we boarded the attack transport, we were given a thorough delousing. Yes, after welcoming us it was the first thing they did for us. At camp we enjoyed another great meal, and after that a good gab fest. Finally, one of the colonels spoke up and said, "Let's go to the movies. We haven't seen one in years." Off we went to the open theater where we sat on planks with the rest of the men. I don't remember what we were watching—we were all so excited. Suddenly over the loud speaker we heard thirteen names called—they were ours. The Lucky Thirteen again were in action. We were to be ready to fly

Japanese Field Hospital Instruments

out at dawn the next morning. That ended our looking at the movie, as we all agreed it would be best to hit the sack and be rested when they would pick us up.

The following morning, just at daybreak as agreed, a truck arrived. We were ready and jumped on for a ride to the airport. Awaiting our arrival was one of the old "flying box cars." We were told this two engine plane had really been their work horse during the war. As soon as we went aboard, the pilot and flight engineer told us we'd be going to Manila. They said the weather was perfect for the flight and we were sure glad to hear that. In this plane the seats ran lengthwise on each side just below the windows, so that we all sat facing each other. It wasn't at all like the passenger planes we were familiar with. As we took off, we noticed the sun was shining on the laps of those sitting on one side of the plane.

About one hour in flight, the engineer came into our section and looked out of the window at the starboard motor. He then returned to the pilot. At about the same time we noticed a strange vibration and someone called attention to the fact the sun was no longer on our side, but was shining on the laps of those across from us. Suddenly we realized the plane must have turned around. The ranking colonel got up, went into the cockpit and talked to the pilot. All of us sat anxiously wondering what was happening. He came back and said we were returning to Okinawa, as we had lost all the oil in the starboard motor. We would have to crash land with just the one motor. It was a terrifying bit of news. We prayed that we'd remain the "Lucky Thirteen."

When we got over the airfield and were preparing to land on one of the coral runways, we saw ambulances and fire trucks dashing along on the runway. It was chilling.

This pilot proved to be extraordinarily skilled as he set that clumsy looking, disabled plane down so softly we hardly knew we were back on the ground. What a relief! We piled out in a hurry and just sat along the side of the runway with the water just below our feet. All were relieved, to say the least.

Suddenly, celebrating our survival, one colonel opened up his duffel bag and brought out a bottle of Old Grand Dad. He opened it up, took a drink, and passed it along the line of thirteen. When the last man got it, there was just enough for one good drink. It seems like we finished that bottle in record time.

Finally, another truck came to pick us up. We thought we'd probably leave the next day. But no, there was another plane sitting near the tower with its motors running. No rest or even intermission after that dangerous adventure. They loaded us into that plane immediately and off we went again. This time the trip to Manila was uneventful. It was a beautiful day for flying but we hardly enjoyed it after what had just happened to us. We were only really happy when we landed safely at Manila International Airport. From there we were taken to a repatriation camp near what I believe to be the barrio of Santa Rosario. We were all assigned to various tents. That finally split up the "Lucky Thirteen."

Chapter 32

A Surprise Visitor

"Valour lies just halfway between rashness and cowardice."

Cervantes

was resting in my tent one day when the flap opened, and my friend, First Sgt. Calm of my old Scout unit walked in. I jumped up and we hugged each other. First he told me he wished we'd have gone with him to the head hunters. He said he'd made it all the way without any trouble. They'd taken care of him when he reached them including giving him the medicine he needed. I must admit he looked much better than when we'd parted in the jungle. We talked at length about our assorted frightening experiences. He said squads of Japanese tried to invade the head hunter country, but never succeeded. Even though they posted sentries at night, when dawn came, the sentries were found with their heads cut off. The head hunters were masters in the use of a bolo, the almost two foot knife which looked like a huge carving knife or a short bladed hatchet. It served them not only for killing, but also to slash their way through the jungle. The head hunters were very short— just like pygmies—but extremely strong and wiry. They could move through the jungle and never make any noise. Sergeant Calm and I parted with tears. Twenty-five years later, when I returned to the Philippines, I found his name in the military cemetery near Los Banos.

As I remained in camp, I found out that my dear friend "Blinky" had recommended me for a special flight which was to go to Singapore, India, Turkey, Spain, Germany, and finally end in Florida. The idea was that people, who were recommended to make this special flight, could later say they had been once around the world. When I found out I was scheduled for it, I could only think of my wife who would be waiting in San Francisco, while I landed in Florida. That would be hard to explain under any circumstances. I had to get off this flight, so I went to Transportation headquarters and asked them to take my name off the roster. I was told that under no conditions could they do that because a General had recommended me.

Off I went in search of the General tent area. When I found the General I thanked him, but when I explained the problem, he understood, and he got me off the roster. The Generals and senior officers were flown out ahead of us to San Francisco. It was then that the General located my wife, Louise, and entertained her along with his family.

In front from left to right: General Bluemel, Louise, Mrs. Bluemel

Chapter 33

The Marine Shark

"Courage is resistance to fear, not absence of fear."
Mark Twain

bout three weeks later, a ship arrived in Manila which was named the Marine Shark. It was on her maiden voyage out of Seattle; from there it was to go to Yokohama and then to us in the Philippines. This was the ship that was to take us home. It was new and we speculated that at some later date, it could be converted to a passenger liner.

When we first left Manila we sailed through the Straits of Magellan in beautiful, calm waters until we finally were out in the then serene Pacific Ocean. One day I was lying on the deck with my friend Boxie. We were sunning ourselves and talking over old times when all of a sudden there was a terrible sound and the entire ship shook. All I could think of was we had hit a mine. Yet the water was so quiet and peaceful that any skipper could have seen a floating mine. Boxie jumped up and started running for a ladder. Down he went, yelling back to me that he knew what had happened. As he shouted I leaned over the side of the rail and looked down into the water to see if the ship was sinking.

Prior to the war, Boxie had been a chief engineer for the American Export Lines. After what seemed like a hundred years, he returned. Meanwhile, I was still watching to see if the ship was slowly sinking. He told me how lucky we were. The engineer on duty was a Third Engineer who was watching water levels in the gauges that show water amounts for the turbines. He hadn't seen a level in one of the gauges and assumed it was full when, in reality it was empty. The turbine had overheated and blew up. Catching his breath, his face white, Boxie said, "I didn't know why the ship didn't split in half." I remember his final words: "I will never know why it didn't happen."

We proceeded with the one turbine, but at a much slower speed, until we reached Pearl Harbor. When we docked a group of top Navy brass boarded our ship. They departed after a bit with the Third Engineer, and we never found out if there were repercussions.

You can imagine the excitement we felt when we were told we'd be leaving Pearl Harbor and proceeding to San Francisco. There were a few problems—the owners of the ship wanted us to go to Seattle, but our brass finally prevailed, getting us routed to San Francisco. As we proceeded to dock, I spotted my faithful wife waiting and waving at me. The dock was full of people there for reunions so it was difficult to find your loved one.

After debarking, some moments stay in memory forever. When we first saw each other, we were not the only ones with tears all over our faces. When I was told to check in at Letterman General Hospital, of course, Louise went with me. I was lucky to have been given a fourteen day furlough and Louise had made arrangements for us to stay at the Fairmont Hotel. When those two blissful weeks were over, I was ordered to report to the Mayo General Hospital at Galesburg, Illinois for my complete physical examination. Following that, I was discharged from active duty, but remained in the Inactive Army Reserve (not at my request either).

Finally Reunited

Chapter 34
After the Return

"There never was a good war or a bad peace"
Benjamin Franklin

When *Louise and I* finally returned to Chicago, my former associate in Milwaukee, Dr. Karl Schlaepfer, wanted me to rejoin him in practice. I told him I wanted to try for a suitable residency so that I might complete my requirements for the examinations in surgery. He understood and even wrote a letter in my behalf recommending me for a job. This was now late fall, and to find a residency was tough, as all appointments had already been made early in spring and summer.

Louise prevailed on me to apply to the Veterans Administration Hospital at Hines, a suburb of Chicago. I made an appointment with the Chief of Surgery, Dr. Charles Puestow who interviewed me saying that one residency in surgery was available. During the questioning he found out I'd graduated from the medical school at the University of Wisconsin at Madison. He asked if I knew his brother who worked there. I replied that I did and had worked under him in the Outpatient Clinics at the University Wisconsin General Hospital. That seemed to have pleased Dr. Puestow. It was then that I felt I had passed my interview. However, he told me I would have to be interviewed by a Dr. Graham at Northwestern University Hospital and by a Dr. Cole at the Medical School of the University of Illinois. I made immediate appointments for interviews with them.

The following morning I saw Dr. Graham and during the interview he asked whom I had worked with in Milwaukee. When I told him Dr. Schlaepfer, he got excited and said, "Karl?", and I answered to the affirmative. He then told me they'd been residents at John Hopkins University Hospitals. We talked a while about Karl. When I finally left, I thought I had this interview on my side. That afternoon, I visited Dr. Cole, who acted just the opposite of the previous two. When I was told to go into his room, he never even asked me to sit down. He asked all sorts of personal questions, then telling me there was only one residency left and he felt it should go to a local doctor. He said I should be applying at the VA Hospital in Milwaukee and wanted to know why I was trying to get into the Chicago facility. I remember telling him I wanted to train in the Chicago area because there would be a greater variety of cases than in Milwaukee. As I left this interview, I was downhearted, thinking he was going to go against me. When I saw Louise waiting in the car I told her I could forget that residency as Dr. Cole was probably going to vote against me. As usual she encouraged me and told me not to lose hope.

The next morning I was called at 8:00 a.m. by Dr. Puestow's secretary who said I had received the appointment as Senior Resident in Surgery and how soon could I report? I was there the same day, you can be sure.

This appointment as a Senior Resident came as a happy surprise. Luckily, the training I received as the Senior Resident was just what I needed and I enjoyed every moment of it. One year after my appointment, I was appointed to the Northwestern University Surgical Research Labs. Every Wednesday afternoon I would leave the hospital to go there and conduct research. I was trying to work out a process whereby the human trachea (windpipe) could be replaced by artificial means. One paper was published on this work.

In my rotating through the various branches of surgery, I became most interested in the field of Thoracic Surgery. When I finished my qualifying training to be eligible to take the certification examinations in General Surgery, I asked Dr. Puestow if I could remain as a resident in thoracic surgery, hoping to get qualified in that field. After a few days, I was not given the resident opening, but was named Assistant Chief of Thoracic Surgery. I finished two years of training in that specialty.

Upon my completion of all this training in 1950, one of the consultants in Thoracic Surgery, Dr. George Holmes, made me a fabulous offer to join him in private practice as a partner. He was one of Chicago's leading thoracic surgeons, with offices in the Helena Rubenstein building on Michigan Blvd. He offered to put $20,000 in the bank for my personal use with no pay back. In our work we would split costs and income 50-50. This was better than a dream. I came home all excited and told my wife.

The following morning, when I returned to the VA Hospital, I was told that Dr. Puestow wished to see me. He handed me a telegram from Washington. I was being offered the job as Chief of Surgery at the VA Hospital in

Livermore, California, a 620 bed hospital.

Overwhelmed, I asked for a few days to think it over. Somehow the more I thought about it, the more I leaned towards the Chief of Surgery position. I considered the fact that I could have made a lot more money in Chicago, but would have been home very little, as Dr. Holmes was operating not only in Chicago, but also in Waukegan, Dekalb and Gary. I also thought of all the nice icy roads I'd be driving through on my way to all these hospitals in the winter months. Discussing it with Louise, she replied that it was my decision. "Whichever way you decide," she said, "I'll back you up with no regrets, one way or another."

I took the appointment at the VA Hospital. George told me, after I told him of the decision, that he would give me two years. If at any time within that period I still wanted to join him, the original offer would stand.

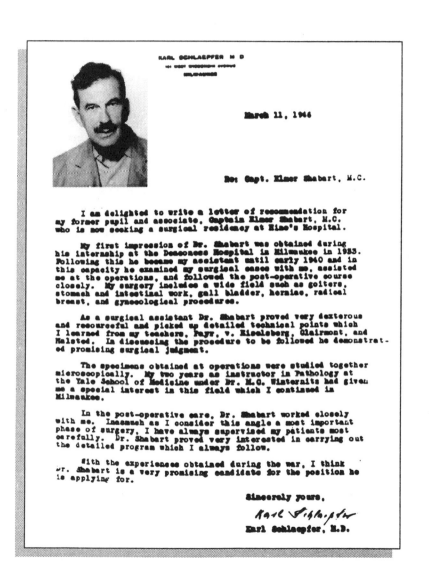

KARL SCHLAEPFER M D
101 WEST WISCONSIN AVENUE
MILWAUKEE

March 11, 1946

Re: Capt. Elmer Shabart, M.C.

I am delighted to write a letter of recommendation for
my former pupil and associate, Captain Elmer Shabart, M.C.
who is now seeking a surgical residency at Hine's Hospital.

My first impression of Dr. Shabart was obtained during
his internship at the Deaconess Hospital in Milwaukee in 1933.
Following this he became my assistant until early 1940 and in
this capacity he examined my surgical cases with me, assisted
me at the operations, and followed the post-operative course
closely. My surgery includes a wide field such as goiters,
stomach and intestinal work, gall bladder, hernias, radical
breast, and gynecological procedures.

As a surgical assistant Dr. Shabart proved very dexterous
and resourceful and picked up detailed technical points which
I learned from my teachers, Payr, v. Eiselsberg, Clairmont, and
Halsted. In discussing the procedure to be followed he demonstrat-
ed promising surgical judgment.

The specimens obtained at operations were studied together
microscopically. My two years as instructor in Pathology at
the Yale School of Medicine under Dr. M.C. Winternitz had given
me a special interest in this field which I continued in
Milwaukee.

In the post-operative care, Dr. Shabart worked closely
with me. Inasmuch as I consider this angle a most important
phase of surgery, I have always supervised my patients most
carefully. Dr. Shabart proved very interested in carrying out
the detailed program which I always follow.

With the experiences obtained during the war, I think
Dr. Shabart is a very promising candidate for the position he
is applying for.

Sincerely yours,

Karl Schlaepfer

Karl Schlaepfer, M.D.

Chapter 35

VA Hospital, Livermore, California

"The great use of life is to spend it for something that will outlast it."

William James

So it was that in *August of 1950* I reported to the hospital and became the Chief of Surgical Services and chief of Thoracic Surgery Service. I was more than ready to put those terrifying POW days behind me. After a period of time, I developed a research lab with help from the Central Office in Washington. In 1953, I was appointed Associate Chief of Professional Services for Research.

Before that, in 1950 and 1952, I had taken the written, oral, and practical exams in general surgery and thoracic surgery. Luckily, I passed all the examinations and became a certified specialist in both fields. As I developed the surgical programs, I began to train residents in surgery and thoracic surgery. Officers were sent to me from the Army Letterman Hospital, the Navy Oak Knoll Hospital, and doctors were sent from the Alameda County Hospital and several local hospitals. I delighted in teaching—my days felt like a reward for having survived.

Colonel French, Chief of Thoracic Surgery at the Letterman Army Hospital, called me one day and invited me over to the hospital in San Francisco, just to "have lunch and get to know each other." While we were eating, several dentists walked by, including the Chief of Dentistry. When Colonel French introduced me to these men, the Chief of Dentistry looked at me and repeated my name, "Shabart?" He asked if I was a former POW, and I replied that I had been one of the involuntary guests of our former enemy. He then asked if I knew General Bluemel. Again I answered that I did. He then said jokingly that he'd always hoped some day to meet this fantastic medical doctor who practiced dentistry as a POW, one who could do things without even instruments. He said that the General had told him to look into his mouth. The inlay I had reinserted was evidently still in place.

We all had a real good laugh after that one. The chief invited me to visit him any time I could be at Letterman. What a surprise for me to hear again about the inlay. Jokingly, I told the Chief he could rest assured I would never practice dentistry again.

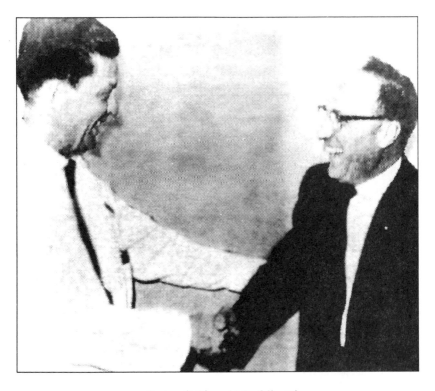

Author (left) and Mr. Olivetti
A broken arm healed

Chapter 36

The Research Investigators

"Life begins on the other side of despair"
Jean Paul Sartre

n the course of my work in researching "Tissue Transplant Rejection," it became obvious that I needed an extremely competent immuno-microbiologist. I was having considerable problems in finding a suitable researcher in this country, even though I was exploring all the leading centers. A friend of mine at the University of California, Davis, called me one day to tell me he thinks he had located a suitable scientist in Japan. Dr. Bankowski, my friend from U.C. Davis, was a world recognized authority in viral diseases in poultry and knew exactly what I wanted. I contacted Dr. Kodama in Japan and asked him to send me a curriculum vitae if he might be interested in my work. He answered yes immediately. I hired him under a three year contract, which was the limit allowed by the U.S. Government.

When my associates and co-workers found out that I had hired a Japanese doctor, after what we had gone through, they thought I had lost my mind! They finally understood that these young scientists were probably only a "glean in their father's eye"—hadn't even been born when we were going through life as POW's. I couldn't hold them accountable and I didn't. Following a three year stint with Dr. Kodama, I subsequently hired Dr. Akira and Dr. Takeuchi for three years each. Eventually we published a paper in regard to transplantation rejection. As the research progressed, I had Dr. Bankowski appointed as a consultant in Research. In 1967, I received my appointment at U.C. Davis as a lecturer in the Clinical Sciences.

While all this was going on, I was persuaded by a number of residents of Livermore to run for the High School Board of Trustees. After much discussion, I decided to run for the office. I won the election and eventually over the years became President of the Livermore Unified High School District Board of Trustees.

Following some articles about me in the local newspapers, a man appeared in my office one day. He walked in waving his arm, saying, "Do you remember me, Doc?" He'd been a POW during the war and then told me about how he'd fallen off a wooden gangplank in Formosa, breaking his arm. He reminded me that I'd set it using only makeshift materials found on the dock. "I did exactly what you told me, Doc and the arm healed great—I never had any problem with it later. We reminisced for quite a while about those days. He kept telling me how grateful he was and how he couldn't understand how the result was so good with only the scrap piece I'd used as a splint. I told him I didn't understand it either. What a good feeling I had! Somehow the local newspaper got wind of the story and took pictures of us greeting each other.

Chapter 37

Another Unexpected Visitor

"I shall tell you a great secret, my friend. Do not wait for the last judgement. It takes place every day."

Albert Camus

Several months after that, the admitting officer called to tell me there was a man in his office who wanted to see only me. He said his name was Baumgartner and had only one arm. I told Mac to send him up immediately. Sure enough, it was good old "Bum." He had no prosthesis and said he never wanted one. He was getting along just fine, except recently when he'd been in a hospital in West Virginia where they told him he had tuberculosis and needed some lung surgery. When he heard that, he told them he had a surgeon friend. If surgery was needed, he was going to go to him. That surgeon happened to be me. How he ever knew I was out in California, I never knew.

I had him admitted and worked his case up. I came to the conclusion that, yes, he indeed needed a lobectomy (removal of a portion of the lung). The operation was done without any complications and he did very well. One day the surgical floor supervisor phoned me to tell me that the "Bum" was missing from bed check. You had to know him—it was just like "Bum" to not follow orders and walk out if it so pleased him. Yes, he was gone. Later

I found he'd left me a short note with the word "Thanks."

One day I received a call from Colonel French that he was sending me a resident named Major Gillespie. When I asked if this officer had a father who was a general, his answer was yes and that shortly after the war ended, General Gillespie commanded Letterman General Hospital. Hearing that, I said, "By gosh, I was a POW with his father. We were good friends." What a strange circumstance that so many years later I should be given the chance to train the son of a fellow POW.

Chapter 38

Afterthoughts

"We few, we happy few, we band of brothers;
For he today that sheds his blood with me;
Shall be my brother."

Shakespeare, 'Henry V'

As I reflect back on Mukden, it is remarkable to me that our mortality rate was so low. I have been told that we had the lowest rate of any Japanese POW camp. Yet I can never forget that many Americans—all at the start of their adult lives—died during the Bataan death march and later. Despite our best efforts during our first year in the Mukden arena we lost in the vicinity of two hundred and twenty men. A great many of these deaths were the result of poor and insufficient rations and disease in Bataan as well as the subsequent ordeals which all the soldiers suffered. The lack of medicines and adequate facilities in Mukden didn't help any either. The rations of soy beans and corn meal, as well as occasional greens that got added later, helped, improving the health of many and cutting down the number of deaths.

Another later development that helped during our long imprisonment, was access to some medicine when finally granted privileges at their army hospital. I have never been able to find out whether such professional courtesy was ever granted at any of the other POW camps.

Putting all these together, along with the dedication of the medical men who tried desperately to do their best with practically no equipment, accounted in the end for the better condition of most of the men towards the end of the war. I think we only lost about fifteen men in our last year of being prisoners of war at Mukden.

Chapter 39
A Speculation

"In time of war the devil makes more room in hell"
German Proverb

he issue of what the twelve Colonels were investigating after all POWs had left camp, brings to mind something I read many years later. I had mentioned how our captors had selected ten men to be taken elsewhere but would not tell our senior officers where. Years later I found out that the Japanese had established Unit 731, relatively close to our camp where atrocious experiments were conducted on human beings. A Gregory Rodriquez, Jr. wrote an article in *The Quan*, a publication of the American Defenders of Bataan and Corregidor and the Journal of Ex American POWs. His article stated that he was able to establish some evidence that Americans were subjected to these vicious experiments. I understand that he is trying, at this time, to get further and complete verification of his findings. Evidently Dr. Ishii, the head of Unit 731, had his assistants inject plague bacilli into Americans. In retrospect I believe the twelve Colonels who were doing some G2 may have been investigating these experiments. U.S. military documents of a Counter Military Intelligence Corps are reported as having uncovered proof that Dr. Ishii had ordered his men to do those hideous injections.

Some POW's to this day maintain they know of similar atrocities conducted in our Mukden camp. If so, it was a well kept secret. It should be remembered we were considered the main camp, and I refer only to that camp since I have no personal knowledge of what happened in any other camps. I know that when we doctors complained to the Commandant that the barracks were full of fleas (we were concerned about plague), he ordered a cleanup of all bedding, and all barracks were sprayed with some sort of chemical to kill the fleas. Did he order that to prevent the plague from spreading among the POW's, or to protect their own skins? Seems like he had some concern for both.

Then too, when the Japanese ordered all men to get shots against typhoid/paratyphoid, there was concern at first by the doctors that maybe they were up to no good. We were suspicious but had no recourse except to follow their orders. All men were inoculated. The Japanese ordered repeat shots every three months until they were suddenly ordered to stop them. If germ experiments were being conducted in our camp, it wouldn't have made sense that our captors would take the precautions I just mentioned.

In 1995 six former Japanese members of Unit 731 wrote a book about atrocities such as germ injections, human surgical experiments without anesthesia when they had it, and intentional exposure to anthrax and other grave diseases.

I was troubled to find Mr. Rodriquez stating that the Army of Occupation never prosecuted any of the people

involved at Unit 731, not even Dr. Ishii. It is claimed that
a deal was struck: no prosecutions in exchange for all the
data obtained in these horrifying experiments, including
getting help from Dr. Ishii in helping to set up a germ
research lab at Fort Detrick, MD. Further statements tell
us that the U.S. was concerned that the Russians were
way ahead of us in germ warfare knowledge, and therefore we could use additional help. If true, this information
reminds me of the movie "Outbreak." I have no official
knowledge of any of his, only what I read in *The Quan*
Again, I have to say that as far I know, there were no such
experimental atrocities in our camp. Of the others, I can't
say. I am still haunted by a question—did our ten camp
members who disappeared, wind up at Unit 731?

There is reason to believe that when thirty Japanese
were brought to the War Crimes trials on various charges
in May, 1948, some of the charges involved secret experiments on American POW's. Five were sentenced to
death, four to life imprisonment, and fourteen to lesser
sentences. In September, 1950 most sentences were
reduced, and by 1958 all were free. None were ever exe-
cuted. Although several Japanese who participated in
such experiments have since admitted the atrocities practiced on POW's, they do not specify nationality—were
the POW's all Americans? Were some Russian and
Chinese POW's? It is stated that all evidence of any kind
associated with these atrocities was destroyed after
August 1945.

These are two different versions of what subsequently
happened. That human experiment atrocities occurred is
a simple fact. However, what actually happened is still
impossible to know, especially since all evidence was
destroyed.

Display at Army Medical Museum (Ft. Sam Houston, Texas)

For some time after my return to the States, I tried to find out the fate of the Japanese doctors in the Imperial Hospital, especially the dentist. All I ever found out was they were taken, along with others, to the northern edges of Siberia. Finally, over time, they all expired. How sad, indeed.

Now a reflection on a less charged subject. Way before our capture, when the seven of us sailed out of Fort Mason to go to the Philippines, there was a doctor named Charles Osbourne. He was a very likable chap. Before we set out, his wife went to Shreves Jewelry store in San Francisco, bought him a sterling silver lighter and had it inscribed, "Stolen from Dr. Charles Osbourne." When we landed in Manila, Dr. Osbourne was assigned to a base on the island of Mindanao. It is said that he either died or, more likely, was killed when the Japanese invaded the island. When the American Marines invaded the Island of Guadalcanal, in the course of the fighting, an American Marine came across a dead enemy soldier. Something possessed him to search the man and, as he did, he found in his pocket a sterling silver lighter inscribed, "Stolen from Dr. Charles Osbourne." What a strange event. The Marine gave it to his commanding officer, who saw to it that the lighter was shipped to Command Headquarters in Australia. From there a report was made to Washington. Mrs. Osbourne was contacted and they asked her to describe a cigarette lighter that could possibly have belonged to her husband. When she accurately did so, they returned the lighter to her. She then knew too well that her beloved husband was probably dead. It still hurts to remember lost lives. All those good people gone.

Now for the two boxes of Japanese Army Instruments.

After retaining them for those fifty years, I put them to rest by donating them to the Army Medical Museum at Fort Sam Houston, Texas. Their viewers can always reflect on the irony that they were there all the time I agonized about doing surgical procedures with no decent equipment.

Chapter 40

A Final Thought

"Each man must for himself alone decide what is right and what is wrong, which course is patriotic and which isn't. You cannot shirk this and be a man."

Mark Twain

ever in my wildest dreams did I ever think that, as I sat and wrote this book, the events occurring when I was a POW and during the Bataan death march, would return so vividly. In documenting my thoughts, it seemed to me I was just reliving yesterday. Now I ask the reader, after finishing this story, "Do you think I lived up to the purpose in life presented in the anonymous poem at the beginning?" I can only say I have lived a full and fulfilling life. Unlucky in war (those years were grim), I was lucky in love—my wife, Louise not only stood by me always, but encouraged me in everything I tried.

I will also always be grateful to Major General Keith Simmons, of the Royal British Service; Major General H. de Fremery of the Netherlands Royal Colonial Army and the following American officers: Major General George Moore, Commander Phillipine-Ryukus Command; Major General Edward Witsell, Adjutant General as ordered by the Secretary of War, Brigadier

General Clifford Bluemel, Colonel Wibb Cooper, Chief Surgeon United States Forces in the Philippines, Lt. Colonel John Pugh, Aide de Camp to General Jonathan Wainwright, and my special teacher, Dr. Karl Schlaepfer in Milwaukee. I want also to recognize Colonel F. R. Grimwood, British Army, who took the time to write me and tell me that the operation I performed on him for the unusual bowel obstruction kept him well. To all these and many more, too numerous to mention, I give my heartfelt thanks. Having lived through the Bataan death march all those years ago, I've been grateful for life itself ever since.

Dr. & Mrs. Shabart

Illustrations

Original Documents

Mukden Prisoners of war camp
August 15th 1945

To anyone who is interested.

For already more than two years Dr. Elmer Joseph Shabart has been functioning as main chirurgical physician in the above quoted camp where too he is charged with the external treatment of the outdoor patients.

Undersigned has been under his treatment since the day of his arrival here at the end of May. Personally I am more than satisfied with the really wonderful improvement he has obtained of the ailment of which I have been suffering for more than three years. This the more amazing because of the lack of adequate equipment combined with the Japanese reluctancy to allow the foreign doctors the necessary independancy of action.

P. o. w. doctors not only have to know how to handle their patients but even more how to deal with Japanese mentality.

It was however in first instance after the deplorable accident which occurred when in December of last year this camp was hit by several bombs which caused several deaths and wounded that Dr Shabart showed his capacity as leader. When the Japanese medical staff lost their heads Dr. S. immediately took charge of the situation. In a very short time he had the nearly so heavily wounded transported to the hospital thanks to his capable and quick treatment all of these - safe one - were saved though several amputations had to be performed.

Based on what I have seen and heard of Dr. Shabart's work here, I think that he has proved himself capable as man and physician to take on his shoulders the responsible task of the care of a hospital.

[signature]

Major [illegible]
U.S. [illegible]

Muk en, Manchuria,
August 20, 1945.

SUBJECT: Commendation.

TO : Lieutenant General J. M. Wainwright,
United States Army.

1. This communication is to bring to your attention 1st Lt. Shabart, 45th Infantry, (P.S.). Shortly after the fall of Bataan and Corregidor Dr. V. T. Shabart was taken to a Japanese prison camp at Mukden, Manchuria where he has remained during the entire period of his captivity. Placed in this location along with approximately 1600 enlisted men and 30 officers both American and British, his duties have been arduous and exacting. As is known by all who have come in contact with the Japanese military, work under their supervision for the benefit of fellow prisoners is at best trying and is often impossible. Even though incoming drugs and medicines are international Red Cross issues, Japanese authorities treat them wholly as Japanese property, issuing them either not at all or in ridiculously minute amounts. Operating under conditions most adverse Dr. Shabart has worked methodically, diligently, patiently.

2. During December of last year this prisoner of war camp was bombed by American planes, during which bombing many prisoners were killed and over 60 were wounded. Of the last named group Dr. Shabart saved all but one, inspite of the fact that many of the operations were intricate and difficult. In view of the extent of these bomb injuries such a record appears miraculous, but on closer examination the untiring and unceasing work of Dr. Shabart is apparent. Since the above incident the Japanese medical authorities have given Dr. Shabart a free hand, to the best of my knowledge an almost unprecedented in Japanese prisoner of war camps. Such was their respect for this young doctor and surgeon.

3. Upon the arrival of the undersigned in this camp on April 29, 1945, the praise of the men for this doctor was universal and continuous. All concerned give him the highest praise. After 4 months of observation as a fellow prisoner I realize why. It is deserved.

4. In my opinion the comparatively good health enjoyed in this camp is in large part due to the untiring efforts of Dr. Shabart. He has proved himself a hard worker, and outstanding surgeon, a capable administrator.

Compared with the work of other army doctors and surgeons, who I have observed during this most trying and difficult life of a prisoner of war, Lieutenant Shabart's work has been of the highest calibre, and under the circumstances beyond the call of duty, and therefore worthy of commendation and a possible decoration.

John Ramsey Pugh
JOHN RAMSEY PUGH,
Lt. Col. (Cav) Aide-de-Camp

IN REPLY REFER TO S. G. O.

WAR DEPARTMENT
OFFICE OF THE SURGEON GENERAL
WASHINGTON

To whom it may concern:—

Captain Elmer J. Shabart arrived in the Philippines a short time before the beginning of the war with Japan. He was stationed on Bataan and shortly thereafter was sent to Manchuria as one of the medical officers accompanying a group of prisoners of war.—

I am not familiar with Capt. Shabart's professional background but upon arrival in Mukden in the summer of 1945 I became familiar with the work that he had done and

IN REPLY REFER TO S. G. O.

WAR DEPARTMENT
OFFICE OF THE SURGEON GENERAL
WASHINGTON

was then doing in the Mukden Camp. He was the operating surgeon for the camp and had shown unusual ingenuity and resourcefulness in the organization of the surgical service under very trying conditions.—

He is capable, industrious and in my opinion possesses both administrative and professional ability much above the average.

M. E. Cooper
Colonel, MC
formerly Chief Surgeon U.S. Forces in China

Hope this find you OK I'm
doing pretty good. Take Care
& Have a Merry Christmas
      &
   Happy New Year
This is my good time of the
year. Last time I saw you
was 1945. And so I say
   Thank God somebody got
      us Home

Wishing You
An Especially Nice Christmas!

Peter Lack P.o.W
7 June

Hoten Camp - Mukden
Manchuria
17. 8. 1945 -

Lieutenant Elmer J. Shabart Medical
Corps of the United States Army has
attended the British Prisoners of War
during their period of imprisonment in
Mukden - during that period he performed
more than one major operation. The British
Officers and other ranks are very grateful
for his valuable services and his
invariable readiness to assist them at all
times -

F. Keith Simmons
Major General
British Service -

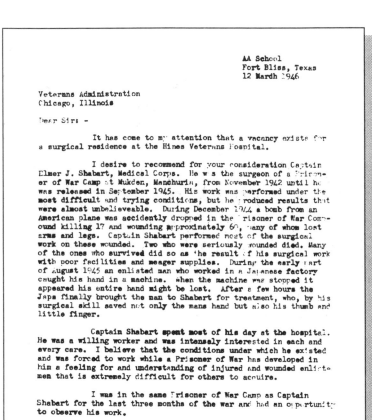

AA School
Fort Bliss, Texas
12 March 1946

Veterans Administration
Chicago, Illinois

Dear Sir: -

It has come to my attention that a vacancy exists for a surgical residence at the Hines Veterans Hospital.

I desire to recommend for your consideration Captain Elmer J. Shabart, Medical Corps. He was the surgeon of a Prisoner of War Camp at Mukden, Manchuria, from November 1942 until he was released in September 1945. His work was performed under the most difficult and trying conditions, but he produced results that were almost unbelieveable. During December 1944 a bomb from an American plane was accidently dropped in the Prisoner of War Compound killing 17 and wounding approximately 60, many of whom lost arms and legs. Captain Shabart performed most of the surgical work on these wounded. Two who were seriously wounded died. Many of the ones who survived did so as the result of his surgical work with poor facilities and meager supplies. During the early part of August 1945 an enlisted man who worked in a Japanese factory caught his hand in a machine. when the machine was stopped it appeared his entire hand might be lost. After a few hours the Japs finally brought the man to Shabart for treatment, who, by his surgical skill saved not only the mans hand but also his thumb and little finger.

Captain Shabart spent most of his day at the hospital. He was a willing worker and was intensely interested in each and every care. I believe that the conditions under which he existed and was forced to work while a Prisoner of War has developed in him a feeling for and understanding of injured and wounded enlisted men that is extremely difficult for others to acquire.

I was in the same Prisoner of War Camp as Captain Shabart for the last three months of the war and had an opportunity to observe his work.

CLIFFORD BLUEMEL
Brig General USA

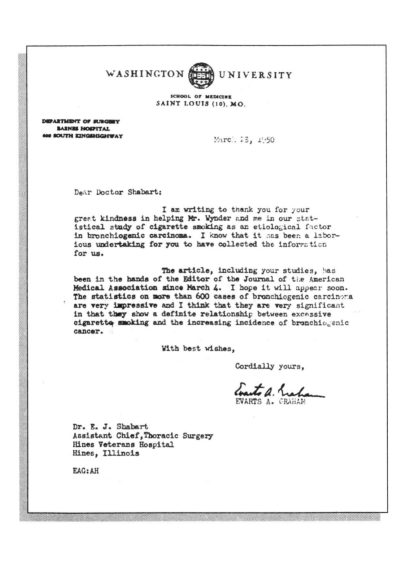

WASHINGTON UNIVERSITY

SCHOOL OF MEDICINE
SAINT LOUIS (10), MO.

DEPARTMENT OF SURGERY
BARNES HOSPITAL
600 SOUTH KINGSHIGHWAY

March 23, 1950

Dear Doctor Shabart:

I am writing to thank you for your
great kindness in helping Mr. Wynder and me in our stat-
istical study of cigarette smoking as an etiological factor
in bronchiogenic carcinoma. I know that it has been a labor-
ious undertaking for you to have collected the information
for us.

The article, including your studies, has
been in the hands of the Editor of the Journal of the American
Medical Association since March 4. I hope it will appear soon.
The statistics on more than 600 cases of bronchiogenic carcinoma
are very impressive and I think that they are very significant
in that they show a definite relationship between excessive
cigarette smoking and the increasing incidence of bronchiogenic
cancer.

With best wishes,

Cordially yours,

Evarts A. Graham
EVARTS A. GRAHAM

Dr. E. J. Shabart
Assistant Chief, Thoracic Surgery
Hines Veterans Hospital
Hines, Illinois

EAG:AH

UNITED STATES ARMY

PHILIPPINES—RYUKYUS COMMAND

OFFICE OF THE COMMANDING GENERAL

APO 707

SEP 29 1

Mr. Elmer J. Shabart
1653 W. Division St.
Chicago, Illinois, USA

Dear Mr. Shabart:

A letter has been received from Mr. Charles G. Hollingsworth, a former Prisoner of War, informing me of the services you rendered while a Prisoner of War in Manchuria and the Philippines to Prisoners of War, and to the cause of the United States, the Philippine Commonwealth and Allies during the recent war.

Since I believe you will appreciate having this letter, I have had copies made and am enclosing one of them for you.

I personally desire to express my appreciation for the splendid services you have rendered.

Sincerely,

GEO. F. MOORE
Major General, U. S. Army
Commanding

1 Incl:
Copy of letter from Mr. Charles G. Hollingsworth.

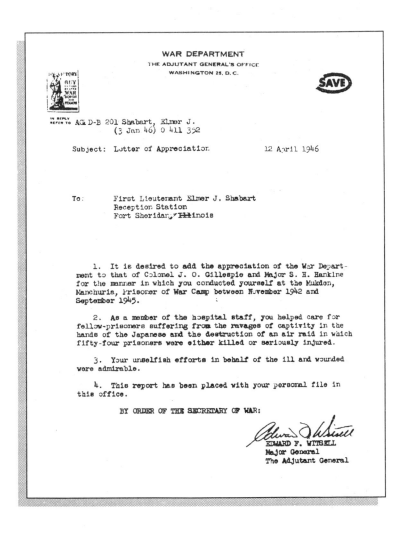

WAR DEPARTMENT
THE ADJUTANT GENERAL'S OFFICE
WASHINGTON 25, D. C.

IN REPLY
REFER TO AG D-B 201 Shabart, Elmer J.
(3 Jan 46) O 411 352

Subject: Letter of Appreciation.   12 April 1946

To: First Lieutenant Elmer J. Shabart
         Reception Station
         Fort Sheridan, Illinois

        1. It is desired to add the appreciation of the War Depart-
ment to that of Colonel J. O. Gillespie and Major S. H. Hankine
for the manner in which you conducted yourself at the Mukden,
Manchuria, Prisoner of War Camp between November 1942 and
September 1945.

        2. As a member of the hospital staff, you helped care for
fellow-prisoners suffering from the ravages of captivity in the
hands of the Japanese and the destruction of an air raid in which
fifty-four prisoners were either killed or seriously injured.

        3. Your unselfish efforts in behalf of the ill and wounded
were admirable.

        4. This report has been placed with your personal file in
this office.

            BY ORDER OF THE SECRETARY OF WAR:

                              EDWARD F. WITSELL
                              Major General
                              The Adjutant General

Thousands Of Operations

Hospital Surgery Chief To Retire

By RICHARD BARNETT

Dr. Elmer Shabart, chief of surgery and associate chief of staff at the Veterans Administration hospital, will resign today after "tens of thousands of operations."

Shabart, 58, leaves his work with "sincere regrets" because of ill health. He will spend his retirement in rest and travel with his wife, Louise.

A survivor of the Death March in Bataan during World War II, Shabart is not only a distinguished physician but a prominent Livermore civic leader.

He started his local service by teaching Cub Scouts First Aid because "there was no one else to do it" and capped it by election to the presidency of the Livermore High School Board of Trustees.

Dr. Shabart is one of the first researchers, along with doctors Winder and Graham, to point out "the suspected correlation between heavy cigarette smoking and lung cancer." He did so in a scholarly article published in 1950. He has contributed over 20 other papers to leading medical journals.

As a medical administrator, Dr. Shabart is noted for raising the surgical bed capacity of the Veterans Hospital from 50 to 144. He is a former vice chairman of the Alameda-Contra Costa Emergency Care Committee.

A lecturer in surgery at the University of California at Davis, Dr. Shabart is a specialist on the heart and lungs. Although he is actually a thoracic surgeon, over 30 young residents in several branches of surgery have been given clinical training under his tutelage at the hospital.

DEPARTMENT OF THE ARMY
LETTERMAN GENERAL HOSPITAL
SAN FRANCISCO, CALIFORNIA 94129

In reply refer to: 21 March 1968

E. J. Shabart, M.D.
Chief, Surgical Service
Veterans Administration Hospital
Livermore, California 94550

Dear Doctor Shabart:

    I send my best wishes for a long and enjoyable retirement. I'm
sure that the many young men you have trained will be a lasting tribute
to the years of work you have put in at Livermore.

    We here are most grateful for your assistance and aid in training
Army thoracic surgery residents.

                        Sincerely,

                        ELMORE M. ARONSTAM
                        Colonel, MC
EMA:ehr   Chief, Department of Thoracic &
                               Cardiovascular Surgery

At retirement

ABOUT THE AUTHOR

r. Shabart was born in Milwaukee, Wisconsin in 1909. He attended schools in Milwaukee, then graduated from the University of Wisconsin, Madison in 1930 with the Degree of Bachelor of Medical Science. Following this he received the degree of Doctor of Medicine from the University in 1933. He was associated with Dr. Schlaepfer from 1934-1940, when he entered the service and was captured in the Philippines. After the Japanese surrender, on returning to the States, he continued the practice of surgery, becoming a certified specialist in both general and thoracic surgery. He was elected into the American College of Surgeons, and became a member of the American Broncho Esophagological Society, the American Laennec Society and the Dr. Charles Puestow Surgical Society. He was a member of the American Medical Association, the Alameda Contra Costa County Medical Society, and at one time was Vice Chairman of the County Medical Society Emergency Committee. He was elected to the New York Academy of Science, Who's Who in the West, American Men and Women in Science, and finally to Who's Who in California. He has published over eighteen research papers and at one time was a consulting researcher for the Navy on the project "Blood Freezing for Blood Banks." One of the most important papers was "Cigarette Smoking as a Possible Etiological Factor in Bronchogenic Carcinoma." He participated with Dr. Evarts Graham and Ernest Wynder in evaluating cases of lung cancer submitting about fifty cases to the total of over six hundred. This was the very first paper ever published on the probable connection between cigarette smoking and lung cancer. It was published in 1950 in the Journal of American Medical Association and created considerable controversy and discussion nationwide at that time and for several years. Later the article was selected by the AMA as a "Landmark Article."

A survivor of the infamous "Bataan Death March," he retired from active practice but still serves as consultant and advisor on several boards.